This introduction to St Bernard through the lens of friendship opens up the twelfth-century monastic world of Bernard and of Aelred of Rievaulx and casts light on the struggles and joys of our lives today.

REVEREND DR LIZ CARMICHAEL MBE
Emeritus Research Fellow, St John's College, Oxford

This fascinating and intimate portrayal of Bernard will inspire anyone wishing to explore the essential place of spiritual friendships in forming true disciples of Christ. This book comes as a direct challenge to superficiality in social media relationships and as a much needed re-evaluation of Jesus's command to love one another in Christian community. This is a book for pastors, spiritual directors, soul friends and church historians alike.

NICK SWANSON
Baptist Union Church Minister; Spiritual Direction trainer, Launde Abbey Team; IPCS Pastoral Supervision tutor

Friendship is desperately needed in our church and society today and into this vacuum Jenny Campbell speaks God's life and truth afresh with insight and wisdom.

REVEREND PHIL AND REVEREND ANNE RICHARDSON
Associate Rectors, Farnborough

This book is an extraordinary undertaking—to draw on the wisdom of twelfth-century monasticism to shine a light into the nature of true love and friendship, amidst all the confusion around these core elements of human experience in our postmodern, social media era. Jennifer Campbell's brilliance in the book is how she has curated original material from the letters and reflections of the monks that by and large speak for themselves—and yet speak directly into our own age. We recognise the living presence within them and cannot help but be touched by it. She has done a superb job in making available riches that would have probably stayed buried to many of us, and, with a light touch, organising them in a way that speak directly to us. One cannot read the book and not have one's own experience touched and illumined by the deeply authentic wisdom it contains.

The book will be of particular interest to those who work in spiritual mentoring, coaching and counselling for the grounded insight and subtlety it brings to understanding spiritual and personal growth in relationship and the capacity for love, centuries before the advent of modern psychology. But it is also fascinating for the student of leadership in the postmodern era to see how they fought and struggled to maintain the integrity of their calling in the turbulent politics of the time—sustaining the influence in relationship to speak truth in love even to those in power—again a defining challenge of our own age.

CHRIS BLAKELEY
Director of the St George's House Leadership Fellows Programme at Windsor Castle; Spiritual Direction Tutor

IN SEARCH OF
Friendship

Lessons from a Monastic Tradition

JENNIFER CAMPBELL

Copyright © Jennifer Campbell, 2022

Published 2022 by Waverley Abbey College, an operating name of CWR, Waverley Abbey House, Waverley Lane, Farnham, Surrey GU9 8EP, UK. Registered Charity No. 294387. Registered limited company No. 1990308.

The right of Jennifer Campbell to be identified as the author of this work has been asserted by her in accordance with the Copyright, Designs and Patents Act 1988, sections 77 and 78.

All rights reserved. No part of this publication may be reproduced, stored in a retrieval system, or transmitted, in any form or by any means, electronic, mechanical, photocopying, recording or otherwise, without the prior permission in writing of Waverley Abbey College.

For a list of National Distributors, visit waverleyabbeyresources.org/distributors.

Unless otherwise indicated, all Scripture references are from The Revised English Bible with the Apocrypha. Oxford University Press and Cambridge University Press, 1989.

Excerpts from Charlie Mackesy (2019) *The Boy, the Mole, the Fox and the Horse*, London: Ebury Press. (Penguin Random House UK edition)

Every effort has been made to ensure that this book contains the correct permissions and references, but if anything has been inadvertently overlooked, the Publisher will be pleased to make the necessary arrangements at the first opportunity. Please contact the Publisher directly.

Concept development and editing by Waverley Abbey College.

Cover design and typesetting by Richard Lyall.

Printed and bound in the UK by Yeomans Ltd.

Paperback ISBN: 978-1-78951-388-2

eBook ISBN 978-1-78951-389-9

CONTENTS

ABBREVIATIONS i
FOREWORD ii
PREFACE iii
INTRODUCTION vii

CHAPTER 1: THE ARC OF FRIENDSHIP 1

    Bernard's quest for friendship   4
    Bernard's depth in friendship   17
    Bernard's breadth of friendship   27

CHAPTER 2: THE TRIANGULAR NATURE OF LOVE 46

    Bernard of Clairvaux on loving God   50
    Aelred of Rievaulx on love and friendship   65
    Aelred of Rievaulx on Christ as the third between friends   84

CHAPTER 3: FRIENDSHIP IN THE PUBLIC SQUARE 91

    Bernard as censor in the twelfth century   96
    Bernard as friend in monastic reform   105
    Bernard as God's friend in society   120

CHAPTER 4: FRIENDSHIP IN THE CIRCLE OF ETERNAL LOVE 135

    Bernard on formation in the love of God   140
    Bernard on friendship as formation in the love of God   153
    Bernard on formation within the fellowship of divine love   162

CONCLUSION 180

A NOTE ON GENRE AND MEDIEVAL TEXTS 184
A NOTE ON THE WORKS OF BERNARD OF CLAIRVAUX 186
CHRONOLOGY OF THE LIFE AND TIMES OF BERNARD OF CLAIRVAUX 192

BIBLIOGRAPHY 196

ABBREVIATIONS

Abbreviations of Bernard's Works

Csi	On Consideration
Cver	On Conversion
GFC	On Grace and Free Choice
HUM	On the Steps of Humility and Pride
Le	Letters
LG	On Loving God
LM	Life of Malachy
LS	Lenten Sermon on the Psalm 'He who dwells'
SS	On the Song of Songs
SSS	Sermons for the Summer Season

Abbreviations of works by others

DeT	De trinitate
LA	The Life of Aelred
MC	Mirror of Charity
RB	The Rule of Benedict
SF	On Spiritual Friendship
VP	Vita prima

FOREWORD

This book introduces us to St Bernard of Clairvaux through the lens of friendship. Close reading of Bernard's writings, not least of his letters, brings out the humanity of the saint and reveals the role of human friendship in his life. The author shows how similar are the experiences of this twelfth-century monk, with his needs and joys, hopes and feelings of inadequacy, to our own experiences of relationship in our present world with its pressures and social media. We see how Bernard goes deeper, setting human friendship within the interdependent loves of God, self, and neighbour – and how in doing so he can speak helpfully to us.

The motifs of love and friendship lead to insights into Bernard's life as the author outlines how he became an attractive and prolific recruiter to the reformed monastic life, a revered abbot and founder of numerous monasteries, and a sought-after adviser to spiritual and temporal rulers. It becomes clear how the writings of Aelred of Rievaulx on charity and friendship, initiated at Bernard's command, spring naturally out of the ethos he inculcated.

The book closes with a challenge: to use more fully the wealth of counsel and friendship that is available, for free, within the church; and to recognize the significant role of friendship in our own Christian formation and growth.

Liz Carmichael MBE
Emeritus Research Fellow
St John's College
Oxford
24 October 2021

PREFACE

As a teenager, I remember being given an essay for my English class entitled 'The nemesis of docility.' It was a hard topic and I had to put on my thinking cap. I wrote about the effects of doing nothing and remaining silent in the face of injustice and inhumanity. I argued that a society which buries its head in the sand when there is something rotten in the body politic will face its nemesis: just retribution or punishment, defeated by its own lethargy and passivity. Good citizens who choose to do nothing and say even less can be the unwitting enemies of the best outcome for a community or nation. Decline comes tiptoeing in silently and unobtrusively and, before we know it, we are ensnared, caught napping and overtaken by disastrous events. We must rise up lest we slip into darkness of our own making.

I suspect this youthful idealism is the impetus for the present book. I still hold the view that we are responsible for our inactivity and that a community of people united in common cause for good can be a catalyst for change, overcoming stagnation and retrogression. And this is particularly so for the society of the Church. We are called to be salt and light in the world and to be agents of change. Jesus Christ summons us, not only as individuals but as people together, to make a difference. We cannot retreat and pretend everything is alright. We are to be God's ambassadors—a cost and a privilege. Within the Church, Christians are to stand shoulder to shoulder, strong for one another, to withstand complicity with the world. For the Gospel teaches it is impossible to be both friends with the world and friends of God. This common strength may be forged through suffering, pain and weakness—the marks of the crucified Christ. Here is the heart of genuine and lasting friendship.

IN SEARCH OF FRIENDSHIP

If friendship with one another is integral to a stable fellowship of Christian believers, how might that stability be achieved in a world of online relationships and fickle friendships? It is the task of this book to answer that question. I present Bernard of Clairvaux as a spiritual leader, a mover and shaker of the Church through his indefatigable belief in the love of God as our purpose and delight. I show Bernard as friend to many from all walks of life, but with an earnest and incredible loyalty and compassion for those closest to him, his brother monks.

I show how Bernard arose as the nemesis of stultified monasticism, his youthful exuberance overtaking and superseding the old order—his new order the leaven in the lump of the European Church. The eternal nature of his accomplishment is that, despite his weaknesses and failings, he belongs first and foremost to Jesus his love. His work is permanent. His movement has not ceased, 900 years from its inception.

An idealistic vision? Perhaps. But a Jesus community is always unobtainable in human terms. If we could achieve perfect human relationships we would not need the power of the Holy Spirit. And we know, without a shadow of a doubt, that imperfection always accompanies our efforts. We break down too easily without God. A Jesus community is that for which Christ died, that we may be one, as he and the Father are one, so that the world may believe (John 17:21). This is aspirational and it is always good to aim high.

Waverley Abbey College has a Bernadine legacy across the river in the form of a ruined Cistercian abbey. It has been my experience that students in the Spiritual Formation classes love nothing better than to be let loose, to leave their desks and computers and wander among the ancient stones. We have been out on a cold and frosty early morning, walking through the mist in silence, apart and yet held together in a common bond of peace and well-being. We have worshipped and prayed in what was once the monks' sleeping quarters; we have listened to Bible readings in what was once the chapter house, the meeting room of the abbey; we have walked the perimeter, past the lay brothers' building—Bernard's innovation to

PREFACE

include ordinary folk in monastic life. And if you stop for a moment you can almost hear the voices of the choir near the high altar, marked now by a gnarled giant tree.

My hope is that this text will become a vade mecum (Latin for 'go with me'), a portable guide or handbook, a ready reference on friendship, especially for those studying and examining the therapeutic relationship and the importance of community in spiritual formation. My prayer is that we will recover with vigour and humility the insights of past spiritual giants. My wish is that we will recover with rigour an appreciation for the ancient texts and allow Bernard to build a bridge between his age and ours.

For the writing of this book my thanks must go to Dr Micha Jazz and the Resources Team at Waverley Abbey Trust for provoking my interest to write an academic textbook for students, to help them understand and use primary source material. Our discussion was held—naturally—while walking among the abbey ruins one fine autumn day in 2020. My thanks to Jayne Downey, librarian at Sarum College, Salisbury, who repeatedly renewed the books I required for research over eight months during the period of the pandemic and national lockdown, when college and university libraries were closed to readers.

I am indebted to Carol Bracher, a new-found friend over numerous Zoom meetings during lockdown in 2020, who offered me much-needed peace and quiet to write. Her beautiful home in Harrogate, North Yorkshire, was an inspiration, as were our excursions into the Dales, to the ruins of the Cistercian abbeys of Fountains and Rievaulx. The extraordinary simplicity of Fountains Abbey: the great vaulted roofs and the undecorated pillars and doors still standing as testament to the reformation which was Cistercian architecture. And deep in a tranquil valley the smaller ruins of Rievaulx Abbey: the site of the abbot's house seen to be not remote at the edges of the monastic enclosure but centred at the heart of community, the place the Abbot Aelred held in the heart of his monks—an enduring testimony to his gift of friendship.

Finally, my heartfelt thanks to my very many dear friends,

especially those who supported, prayed for and showed interest in this project: Andy and Juliet Packer, Claire Gwyer, Jill Holt, Christopher and Suzy Miles, Berendean Money-Kyrle, Martin Down, Winston Dickerson, Shirley Mugglestone, Elsa Rapson, Jacky Vella, David and Lesley Brooke, Mim Haggie, Liz Robertson, Jean Stewart, Margaret Mylchreest, Mae Eady, Marion Bell, Phil and Anne Richardson. And many others too numerous to mention, who have prayed and strengthened my resolve. Nevertheless, despite all this practical and spiritual assistance, any matters of infelicitous style, inconsistencies or errors are mine alone.

Jennifer Campbell

INTRODUCTION

The catalysts for this book are twofold: the location of Waverley Abbey College and the place of friendship in a global village. Highly unlikely bedfellows? An initial reaction might be to dismiss this attempted alliance between a twelfth-century monastic order and the state of friendship in the twenty-first century. Allow me to persuade you of an inquiry into two vastly different landscapes in order to tease out a novel, fresh, and enlivening angle on the love of God and the gift of friendship.

We begin with a room with a view. Gazing from a giant casement window of any one of the grand first-floor rooms of Waverley Abbey House—a Grade 2 listed Georgian mansion built in 1725—a somnambulant student in a lecture or a casual visitor to the College will perceive in close proximity immediately beyond the tranquil loop of the River Wey, the ruins of the first Cistercian abbey established in the British Isles in 1128. An abbot and 12 monks landed from Normandy, for indeed the order was imported from France, to initiate an expansive numerical growth to about 200 with approximately 3,600 hectares of land at the time of the dissolution of Waverley Abbey about 400 years later.

Our interest is not in this anglicised interpretation of the order—English Heritage can easily deal with such queries—but to extract from the writings of Bernard of Clairvaux (1090–1153), the leading light of the Cistercian movement, data to stimulate and provoke contemporary thought around God's love and friendship.

Before even contemplating such a study, we shall have to to overcome our prejudices. There is the question of relevance: why on earth *him*, an out-of-date, other-worldly monk? There is the question of gender: he may be purity personified, but Bernard is unmarried and male. There is the question of leadership: can anything be learned from that remote and superstitious century which is not already known and practised today? After all our species has evolved to a higher height and a greater awareness than ever before in civilization, hasn't it? There is the question of his religion: Catholicism. Can anything good come from that monolithic stable? After all, Christian life began with the Reformation, didn't it? And even *that* is suspect—all those denominations. In fact, no religious tradition can ever quite make the grade and we need to go back to the Bible only.

Such objections have some validity. However, lest we throw the proverbial baby out with the bathwater, we should be aware of significant aspects of Bernard of Clairvaux which may well whet the appetite in our age. In our climate of ceaseless change—technology a turbulence for good or ill—such a discussion from the tradition of Christian spirituality is not only vaguely interesting, but vitally necessary lest we fall prey to lesser or inferior ideas about relationship and what constitutes Christian love and friendship.

Bernard of Clairvaux is *the* dominant figure in the twelfth century, whose influence was felt by crowned heads of Europe, popes, clergy, abbots, and the nobility. His personal correspondence of approximately 500 letters testify to his friendships with both men and women—a kind of spirituality which appealed across the board, drawing people from all walks of life to conversion and to meaningful religious vocations. As literary works, many of his spiritual writings are read today almost as poetry for their sublime beauty and spiritual truth. For Bernard, the heart of religious piety is an affair of the heart—dutiful external observances are only an aid to loving God and to loving and serving others. This is the essence of his work as a reformer, as a luminary in the firmament of the monastic world.

Bernard's leadership spearheaded a vast network of new monasteries—national and international—as the Cistercian Order expanded across Europe. His drastic reconstruction of buildings to reflect a proper purity of lifestyle marks out Cistercian architecture as a departure from the flamboyance and extravagance that

INTRODUCTION

characterised monasteries and churches at the time. Not all his religious practices are acceptable to non-Catholics. His dogmatic views may be anathema to liberal theologians.

This book is not the product of a Bernardine academic schooled in the Cistercian way, at home with the intricacies of that unique spirituality. Nor is it the work of a medievalist whose first language is monastic theology and practice. It is the work of a Protestant, Charismatic, Evangelical layperson, theologian and teacher concerned to develop in students and the wider church a robust theology of spiritual friendship retrieved from the writings of Bernard of Clairvaux. Such beacons may be useful to light the path for a sustained and proactive vision of Christian friendship.

Looking out upon the topography of present social networks, an acute analyst might observe the landmarks sticking out as demonstrating a certain fickleness and instability. Culturally, we have ironed out relationships of accountability. We have sacrificed the practice of challenging one another and instead count how many friends who 'like' us. We are not always ready to ask: 'Are you sure about that?' People who give us pause we are able instantly to 'unlike'. Our friendships are counted by 'likes' and, therefore, lack depth and growth. I overheard a young woman at a pavement café excitedly tell her friend that she had 66 new messages on WhatsApp: 'It's my life' she told her bemused companion. There is nothing wrong with a spectrum of relationship which is broad and wide. The problem comes to light with a depth test. Who really knows me? Who holds me in check? Who gets me going? We might call this trend toward superficiality 'flitting friendships'—flitting from one to another, this scent to that colour to this new group—as bees among flowers.

Opposite to the 'flitting relationship' is the 'fitting friendship': the soulmate of romantic love made for me and only me; the relationship turned inwards for my needs, my desires and my future. A closed friendship cocooned against external intrusion does not venture beyond itself (or beyond me and mine). The metaphor extended to an old boys' network or preferential in-group and the problem persists.

IN SEARCH OF FRIENDSHIP

Where is the eternal perspective? Where is the God voice? Where is the mouthpiece for God? Where does God speak?

These points perceived as prevailing in our cultural milieu can be addressed by acknowledging four priorities in friendship. First, accountability in godly friendships, as Christian fellowship and the wider church in its local expression appears to rise and fall on this Behemoth: opting in and out, fickle mood swings in leadership, church hopping and an inability to stick when the going gets tough. Second, people are not islands and Christians are meant to be glue for each other. Not sticking-plaster to paper over the cracks, but honest influencers, God's spokespersons, keeping one another on track and travelling towards God.

Third, friendship may begin with the twos and threes, but must expand into a band of brothers and sisters, a fellowship of believers, a community, a nation—ultimately the world. To achieve God's purposes, Christian friends cannot rely on worldly methods, bending this way and that according to what works, but must take their bearings from the life of the Trinity, as persons in relationship. Christian friends can make a powerful impact together as the kingdom of God in society. Through such activity we find identity and purpose. Self-reflection is not an end in itself but is turned outwards to work in tandem with the sovereign purposes of the Lord.

Fourth, God has created us to have deep relationships with himself and with others. However, such friendship with God and with one another comes neither automatically nor naturally; it is spiritual and must be worked at spiritually. Formative and fruitful practices and habits can help cultivate intimacy with God and one another.

Having set the stage, we turn to the man in the spotlight, the personality behind the initial acceleration of the Cistercian Order. What can we learn from Bernard of Clairvaux? To be clear, this is not an historical survey, though significant facts have been included. This is not an overview of the works of Bernard of Clairvaux, although it may seem to be a whistle-stop tour of some of his corpus.

INTRODUCTION

Neither is it a biography, though details of his life emerge. This is not an analysis of the spiritual life of the monastery or Bernard. Nor is it a critique of medieval monasticism, though controversial matters will not be avoided. This is not a sociological or psychological classification of the monk per se, though there may be elements which relate to these fields of social science. This is not a study of Bernard's theology, though theological questions will be addressed as they arise.

I have presented Bernard by thematic analysis of original texts covering love and friendship, using primary sources in translation, interspersed with comment and evaluation. Bernard is allowed to speak for himself, as a man of his times—his quirkiness, his failures, his successes, and his gravitas—as an echo chamber for our own age. Points of difference and similarity can go a long way toward answering an underlying question: Why should I bother with these old texts, I am pushed for time and prefer small soundbites?

Four chapters cover the four components of love and friendship: relational accountability, God between friends, friendship as influence for the kingdom of God and the spiritual habits of loving relationship with God and others. Each chapter is allotted a geometric symbol: the arc, the triangle, the square and the circle.

Chapter 1 draws an an arc of friendship reaching from the monastic world to our postmodern era. An arc also connects Bernard with his friend, or friends, and family. We examine three aspects of Bernard's friendships: his quest for friendship; the depth of his friendships; and the breadth of his friendships. From the texts we discover monastic accountability in the give and take of relationships in the enclosed world of community.

Chapter 2 defines friendship in the love of God by means of a divine triangle: the three persons of Father, Son and Holy Spirit, held together inseparably as the Trinity of love. And also a human-divine triangle, with two people at the base and God at the apex, all held together by bonds of love. This grid of love is illustrated by three discussions from Cistercian spirituality: Bernard on loving God; Aelred of Rievaulx (1110–67) on love and friendship; and Aelred of Rievaulx on Christ as the third between friends. From these texts we gain a clear view of relationship within the love of God and Christ between friends.

Chapter 3 uses the square to depict the power of friendship in the public sphere. Three threads are woven into the public tapestry which is Bernard's outer life outside the monastery: as censor in the twelfth century; as friend in monastic reform; and as God's friend in society. From the texts we discover friendship as vivifying spiritual renewal in places of power.

Chapter 4 traces habit-forming spiritual disciplines as a dynamic circle in perpetual motion of love of God and others. Three aspects of the formation of the inner life are considered: formation in the love of God; friendship as formation in the love of God; and formation in the fellowship of divine love. From the texts a pattern emerges of practices developed and maintained by the love of God and love for others.

The book concludes by drawing together pertinent points, carefully suggesting a way forward that may confirm, alter, even radically shift, our worldview.

Chapter 1

THE ARC OF FRIENDSHIP

'What do we do when our hearts hurt?' asked the boy.
'We wrap them with friendship, shared tears and
time, till they wake hopeful and happy again.'

As we begin a study of friendship in the writings of Bernard of Clairvaux, it is necessary to remind ourselves that the world of monastic friendship in twelfth-century Europe is almost a millennium away from our own twenty-first century and, therefore, very different. So completely beyond our ken is this plane of existence that, at a cursory glance, a contemporary, postmodern reader might easily dismiss its archaisms as too eccentric and otherworldly to be of any useful importance today. It is the contention of this chapter to show that, to the contrary, serious engagement with the text will uncover features common to everyone for, intrinsic to the human condition are the feelings of need and our longing to love and to be loved.

In this chapter we shall attempt to construct an incredible arc reaching from that century to this, from that peculiar worldview to our own age. This is our first task: to draw from certain of Bernard's writings—his wide-ranging oeuvre of letters, sermons, and treatises—the sentiments and expressions of emotion, anxiety, pain, loss, and affection common to all human beings everywhere and at all times. At the same time we should be aware that, although we are examining Bernard's thinking about love and friendship in general terms, we are also dealing with a particular man in his own right, sensitive to his own heart and the hearts of others. Our second task is to measure out an arc which passes from one person to another in the adventure of finding love and friendship in earthly terms. We shall think about Bernard at one end of the arc and his friend, or friends at that particular moment, at the other. What passes between them, how they relate, how love is given and received will be the object of our observations.

These two tasks will not be considered under separate headings but working together will assist to inform and underline the progression of the chapter. The chapter will be advanced along three lines: Bernard's quest for friendship in intimate relationship; his depth of friendship expressed in affective language; and, his breadth of friendship with a diverse range of people.

Before we settle to a consideration of Bernard himself under these categories, we should understand the spiritual background against which he wrote about love and friendship.

An arc back to the colossus who was Augustine of Hippo (354–430), theologian and monk, shows the apparent tensions within the discourse on friendship in the early Christian record. Carmichael points out that Augustine did more than any other Western writer to embed love as the foundation for Christian ethics, and his works as a source for the tradition of friendship but concludes that 'his doctrine of love is not wholly hospitable to friendship' (2004: 55; cf. McGuire 2020: 126). The following excerpts from Augustine's *Confessions* are an indicator as to why this might be the case, as they reveal that the testing and temptations of youth are a distraction from doing good and finding God. Such friendship pitfalls are to be avoided by the older and wiser convert to Christ.

Confessions
The guilty pleasure Augustine finds in stealing fruit is that it is done

with friends, boys together in a 'sport, which, as it were, tickled our hearts ... alone I had never done it' (2.9.17, trans. Pusey, 1901: 30). The power of love for the needs of a young errant: 'For there is an attractiveness in beautiful bodies ... and in bodily touch' (2.5.10: 26). Kindred studies knit together intellectual truth-seekers and Augustine the teacher leads his student astray in pagan philosophy: 'I had made one my friend, but too dear to me, from a community of pursuits, of mine own age, and, as myself, in the first opening flower of youth ... I had warped him also to those superstitious and pernicious fables [Manichaeanism].' He confesses to replacing God's love with the love of friends: 'For what restored and refreshed me chiefly, was the solaces of other friends, with whom I did love' (4.8.13: 59).

In summary, friendship for Augustine pre-Christ and without God must not only be reciprocated at every turn but can torment with great sorrow at death:

> This is it that is loved in friends; and so loved, that a man's conscience condemns itself, if he love not him that loves him again, or love not again him that loves him, looking for nothing from his person, but indications of his love. Hence that mourning, if one die, and darkenings of sorrows, that steeping of the heart in tears, all sweetness turned to bitterness; and upon the loss of life of the dying, the death of the living. (4.9.14: 60–61)

At his conversion to the Christian faith, Augustine translates his classical pagan beliefs into a new ideal for true friendship. He cannot live without his friends and his vision of community at Hippo is attractive: an all-inclusive Christian community which embraces all the redeemed in Christ (McGuire, 2020: 126; Carmichael, 2009: 58). However, as a governing universal spiritual principle, all the brothers become friends rather than accepting particular friendships among them. It appears that Augustine is brought to this cul-de-sac because he is conflicted by a two-way system of loving God *and* loving another. The first commandment must precede the second and, unlike in the days of his heathen lusts, his love for God must be paramount. Besides, there is the long view of Christian friendship which never suffers the loss of parting by death: it is bound to the blessed life to come. For Augustine, human friendship—even that within the circle of Christ's love—is always subsumed under love for God.

A small loophole in this argument allows for someone by God's grace to aid for the good another's spiritual journey. Here friendship is used by the Holy Spirit. Thus, friendship is not simply encompassed by divine love but is an integral part of the journey to divine love. As we shall see in Chapter 2, the development of this aspect of Augustine's thought was a preoccupation of the Cistercian Aelred of Rievaulx (1110–67) many centuries later (cf. Carmichael, 2004: 68).

The outworking of the human drive for understanding, of being at home in companionship, is a thrilling discovery in Bernard's writings. The fact that this impulse leads friends, who are in intimate relationship with one another, into a closer walk with God is the monastic legacy to be retrieved. The arc from their time to ours has landed firmly in our postmodern era, where organic networks of relationship are often more powerful than traditional institutional church congregations, in which members can be almost clublike, clicking together and bouncing off one another like so many billiard balls.

BERNARD'S QUEST FOR FRIENDSHIP

The following extract from a sermon on the Song of Songs bears out the ardour of love and the lover: the gentle rhythm of love coming and going—the ebb and flow to and from its divine source:

> *I love because I love; I love that I may love. Love is a great reality, and if it returns to its beginning and goes back to its origin, seeking its source again, it will always draw afresh from it, and thereby flow freely. Love is the only one of the motions of the soul, of its senses*

> *and affections, in which the creature can respond to his Creator… Now you see how different love is, for when God loves, he desires nothing but to be loved, since he loves us for no other reason than to be loved, for he knows that those who love him are blessed in their very love.* (Bernard, SS 83.2.4, trans. Edmonds, 1980: 4, 184)

The lover is the one who knows love, which means knowing reality. However, knowing love is not an intellectual knowledge, which assents to a truth, but a powerful straining to arrest and hold with every fibre of one's being. In the treatise On Consideration, Bernard speaks of 'seizing' love:

> *We must strive 'to seize, with all the saints, the length and the breadth, the heights and the depth' [Eph. 3:18]. Paul said 'seize' and not 'know'. We must not limit our search to the areas of reason; we must desire its fruit with all our power. The fruit does not lie in knowledge, but in the act of seizing.'* (Csi 5.13, trans. Sommerfeldt, 1991: 97)

In Bernard the quest to seize love traverses a wide arc from himself to God and back again. In the range of love's action he sees all human love ablaze in the light of the divine love. The journey of love follows an arc of God's love from its reception to the giving of human love.

The treatise De diligendo Deo (On Loving God) is centred around a theme of a 'school of love' and is based on the text, 'We love because he first loved us' (1 John 4:19). Bernard states simply: 'The more surely you know yourself loved, the easier you will find it to love in return' (LG 3.7, trans. Evans, 1987: 179). It follows that to know yourself loved is to be enabled to love yourself. You begin with love for yourself in the flesh and proceed to love for your neighbour, first in the flesh and gradually in a more spiritual way until this love is extended to the whole community of faith. Bernard wants us to see that love as a fleshly, bodily activity is the first step in the progress of human love to divine love (LG 7.23: 191–192).

LONGING FOR LOVE

On paper or in a hypothetical pulpit this notion of the progress of the soul from carnal (or physical) attachments to the refined air of spiritual love seems effortless. Far from it: in the writings of the young Bernard, as in Augustine, there is evidence of conflict, of battles waged in the arena of human and divine love, of a contest of allegiance to God in loving and being loved.

Song of Songs: Sermon 14.4

A motif of love desired and deferred is taken up by Bernard in a sermon on the Song of Songs. Describing to his fellow monks his yearning for the presence of God despite his coldness of heart depicts the very human ache, common to us all, for connection. A poignant picture of numbed feelings presents to the residents of our twenty-first century interconnected global village an arc back to an enclosed community of reclusive brothers. Tremors of our troubled age 'numbed and languid' and unable to engage with a God long forgotten may be found in this piece of poetry:

> *I am not ashamed to admit that very often I myself, especially in the early days of my conversion, experienced coldness and hardness of heart, while deep in my being I sought for him whom I longed to love [Song 3:1]. I could not yet love him since I had not really found him; at best my love was less than it should have been, and for that very reason I sought to increase it, for I would not have sought him if I did not already love him in some degree. I sought him therefore that in him my numbed and languid spirit might find warmth and repose.* (SS 14.4.6, trans. Walsh, 1971: 1, 102)

From deep within that closed community of God-seekers comes a heartfelt cry, a raw and wretched reaching out for a flesh-and-blood person, as an isolated Bernard bears his heart to his fellow monks, as

> *nowhere could I find a friend to help me, whose love would thaw the wintry cold that chilled my inward being, and bring back again*

> the feeling of spring-like bliss and spiritual delight. But my languor and weariness only increased, my soul melted away for sorrow, even to the verge of despair. All I could do was repeat softly to myself: 'Who can stand before his cold?' [Psa. 147:17]. (14.4.6: 102)

There is an inkling of self-pity, perhaps even of self-mortification or abasement when a little comfort comes through a holy friend. It is not enough! Bernard longs for more than a 'mere puff of perfumed air' from an anointed person in passing, or the memory of a deceased or absent friend. He is happy to have the experience of a human intermediary sent by God but wishes the encounter to be more telling, a 'dewy sprinkling' which touches him humanly.

> Then, at times when I least expected, at the word or even the sight of a good and holy man, at the memory of a dead or absent friend, he set his wind blowing and the waters flowing, and my tears were my food day and night. How can I explain this? Only by ascribing it to the odour from the oil that anointed the friend in question. For me there was no anointing, but rather the experience that came by another's mediation. And so, though made happy by this favour, I was also embarrassed and humiliated: it was a mere puff of perfumed air, not the dewy sprinkling for which I longed. Given only the pleasure of its odour and not of its touch, I saw myself as unworthy of him to whom God himself would communicate his sweetest joys. (14.4.6: 102–103)

Bernard then pours forth his unquenched desire for plain human friendship, not given as assisted grace from God but by the person himself. He is conflicted in his embarrassment that the sweet recollection of a grace-filled friend should be his succour rather than God himself. The sentiment touches on the human longing for companionship on the journey to God:

> And even now, if a similar experience should happen to me, I eagerly grasp at the proffered gift, I am grateful for it, even though I feel sad

> *beyond words, that I have not won it by my own merits, that despite my urgent requests it has not passed directly from his hand to mine. I feel ashamed that the remembrance of human goodness should affect me more powerfully than the thought of God.* (14.4.6: 103)

Bernard closes this open-hearted part of the sermon with the following injunction to the listening brothers. They are to have the wisdom to accept that such divinely appointed moments of human fellowship are given by God to heal and free the seeking soul:

> *Many of you too, I feel, have had similar experiences, and have them even still. In what light then must we view them? I hold that through them our pride is shown up, our humility guarded, brotherly love fostered and good desires aroused. One and the same food is medicine for the sick and nourishment for the convalescent; it gives strength to the weak and pleasure to the strong. One and the same food cures sickness, preserves health, builds up the body, titillates the palate.* (14.4.6: 103)

Clearly Bernard's warmth and affection for his brother monks overflows with pastoral concern that they hold fast in expectancy of God's nudges and prompts through fellow pilgrims journeying on the way of holiness. Fenced in as they were with one another in a subdued monastic enclave, it is easy to see how a glance, a chance meeting, a wise remark, an understanding smile, or greeting might inspire and motivate. Here is the outworking of Augustine's vision of brotherhood in a community of redemption. The question arises as to whether Bernard is offering more than this in his quest for friendship, more than the convention of monastic friendship in foregoing centuries.

In his recent and enlightening biography on the inner life of Bernard, McGuire points out that in Augustine and other Church Fathers there is 'an element of hesitation, a questioning of the value of bonds of friendship', but with Bernard there are 'no second thoughts' (2020: 126). To express affection towards those dear to us is not only human but necessary. This sentiment of a human, even physical or carnal manner of love, is the new sensibility in Bernard which McGuire finds to be a turning-point in Western culture, 'transforming the monastic ideal of separation from the world and allowing the tenderness and intimacy of human bonds into the cloister' (2020: 125).

Prior to studying the implications of this fresh dynamic in general terms—in a universal arc from Bernard to many others—is the arc of the particular friendships cultivated which shine a light on the fledgling reform in friendship. The relationship between Bernard and William of Saint Thierry is a case in point.

INTIMATE FRIENDSHIP

William of Saint Thierry (d. 1148), abbot of the Benedictine house that bears his name, was a theologian, spiritual writer and reformer best known as the biographer of Bernard of Clairvaux. He fell under the spell of Bernard at their first meeting and became one of his closest friends. Together the two abbots became hopeful allies for monastic reform. William's wish to join the Cistercian movement brought underlying tensions which were felt in their later friendship (Matarasso, 1993: 107–108; Elder, 2011: 108–116; James, 1998: 125). The spirituality of William and Bernard was embedded in a common goal: the vision of God. They spoke the same language: love is the force which re-forms the human being, a current which redirects the soul away from self-absorption to life in God, so becoming the love of God (cf. Elder, 2011: 128–132).

Recorded in the *Vita prima* is William's frank admiration for the Cistercian discipline and the esteem in which he holds Bernard from the moment he enters the orbit of the 'good-looking, keen-witted, well-mannered, elegant, and aristocratic young man who chose the monastic life when he could have succeeded brilliantly at any worldly career' (trans. and cited in Elder, 2011: 117). Reciprocal affection is exchanged: Bernard writes 'to his dear friend William' (Le 236: 314) and in a letter to a mutual acquaintance discussing his unpublished theological treatise, Bernard explains that he would not at all mind William seeing the piece 'when I would gladly lay bare my whole soul for him to see if I could' (Le 91: 136).

Letter 87

Letters in the monastic world can be very revealing and the correspondence from Bernard to William is no exception. In Letter 87 he truly does 'lay bare' his inner turmoil as he tussles with the exacting demands he feels William is making upon their friendship. Clearly, all is not plain sailing and this particular friendship has gone aground, albeit temporarily. Bernard is somewhat tetchy about William's analysis of their affection for one another. He sets out the argument that only the spirit of a person knows what is in that person, but (with a tone of irony) that William has been able to

> *weigh and mutually to compare our affection for each other, so as to deliver a verdict not only on the state of your own heart, but even on that of another… You may be right when you say that my affection for you is less than yours is for me, but I am certainly certain that you cannot be certain.* (Le 87. 1: 125)

As the letter progresses, it is easy to see at once that Bernard is addressing fundamental concerns often found in all relationships and common to the human state, whatever the age or custom. Especially noticeable in twenty-first century social media are these same hallmarks of insecurity: Have they seen the text? What do they think about me now? How many 'likes' from my Facebook post today? Did I get a 'wave' for my profile? Why haven't they answered my e-mail sent an hour ago?

Bernard is penetratingly brisk, even brusque as he questions William's sulky declaration that 'My affection for you is greater than yours for me' (1: 125). With abbatial expertise he parries with the older abbot, probing for the truth of the accusation:

> *What proof have you that my affection for you is less than yours is for me? Is it, as you aver in the postscript of your letter, that*

*the messengers from here who pass to and fro by you never
bring any token of my good will or affection? What sort of token,
what sort of proof do you expect? Are you worried because I
have not yet answered your many letters to me? (2: 126)*

Bernard's psychological insights into the state of mind of his friend lead him to an outburst of prayer in the letter as he turns in desperation to the Lord who understands all friendships and from whom love comes. How much does he love William? This he cannot tell and this he tells William through the medium of a prayer, attempting perhaps to relieve the tension and defuse the situation:

*O Sun of Justice, whose rays enlighten the hearts of men with
divers graces! Thou knowest and I feel that by thy gift I love
this man for the sake of his goodness. But how much I love
him, that I cannot tell, thou knowest. It is thou, Lord, who
givest the power to love, it is thou who knowest how much
thou hast given him to love me and me to love him. (2: 126)*

Working through his confusion and doubt, Bernard admits that, in the light which God sheds he may indeed be permitted to measure his love for William, but this is only according to and subject to divine favour. Human friendship and love can only be perceived in the greater love which has enfolded and absorbed his life. And this human/divine dilemma leads him to question whether he loves William enough and, whether, in fact, he can lay down his life for his friend—as Jesus did:

*By thy favour I feel that I love this man, but I have not yet the light
to see whether I love him enough. I do not know whether I have yet
achieved that love, greater than which no man can have, whereby
I would be enabled to lay down my life for my friends. (3: 126)*

Bernard seems almost to upbraid himself as, with utter transparency and complete honesty, he thinks about William. The closing words of the letter are the cry of a heart abandoned to Christ, yet searching for human intimacy. Bernard recognises his shortcomings in loving, knowing that he is totally reliant upon divine power to love more. He appeals to William to be content to accept him as he is and not as his friend wishes him to be.

> Woe is me, if (as I greatly fear) I am either loved by this man more than I deserve or love him less than he deserves… And I too, although I love you less than I should, yet I love you as much as I can according to the power that has been given me. Draw me after you that I may reach you and with you receive more fully whence comes the power to love. Why do you try to reach me and complain that you are not able? You could reach me if you but considered what I am; and can reach me still whenever you wish, if you are content to find me as I am and not as you wish me to be. (3–4: 126–127)

Letters 87 and 88 must be seen not only as a literary expression of the limits of personal friendship but read in context. For indeed Bernard is navigating a particularly difficult situation. William wishes to get closer to his friend and has requested that he leave his position as abbot in his Benedictine house to join him at Clairvaux as a lowly Cistercian monk. Bernard's refusal to let him do so precipitates William's rebuke and inspires Bernard to write about boundaries. Despite the upheaval the two men remain friends for life.

Letter 88

McGuire (2020: 47) alights on Letter 88 as a cameo of the twelfth-century predilection among monks and churchmen to find ways of rendering in words their bonds of affection. The salutation which begins the letter is the same phrase as that used by William, deliberately it would seem, in order to confirm the closeness he feels to his friend: 'To his friend all that a friend could wish.' The explanation follows in true monastic convention. Despite the rocky route they have traversed, the absence of the two friends from one another cannot be an obstacle to this friendship:

> It was you who gave me this formula of greeting when you wrote 'To his friend all that a friend could wish.' Receive back what is your own, and in doing so realize that my soul is not far from one with whom I share a common language. (1: 127)

True to form, Bernard encloses these tender expressions of fond love within a wider issue, in this case the pressing problem of a runaway monk who is determined to tarry at Clairvaux and whom Bernard is equally determined to return to his abbot and order. William is instructed to receive him en route with serious words, but also to write to his abbot on his behalf in a humane fashion.

Letter 89

James, the translator of the most recent edition of the letters, inserts Letter 89 as the third in the personal correspondence of Bernard to William of Saint Thierry, although both date and recipient are uncertain. What is eminently and lucidly apparent is Bernard's vulnerability as he weaves his tapestry of words, sketching a scenario in language of the most intimate kind. This epistolary style is one from which we may well learn, as text messages and e-mails can prove to be circuit breakers cutting out communication and causing confusion and misunderstanding rather than clarifying intention. Painstakingly Bernard explains and elucidates his feelings, thereby protecting the friendship rather than cruelly undermining it. Contrary to the throwaway attitude of our age, which can so readily impact on our friendships, he believes that 'true friendship never wears thin.'

> As I drew myself in my letter to you, so I really am; except that I could not express on paper all that I felt in my heart… I do not ask for my friend back, because I am confident that I hold him; I do not receive him back, because I have never lost him. I cling to him, and there is no one who can take him from me. I embrace again as of old my friend because true friendship never wears thin, else it were no true friendship.

> *I shall hold on to him... because you deem me worthy of yourself, I am yours and shall be yours as long as I live.* (128)

The passage is an example in miniature of the beauty of Bernard's language as Casey describes it, the fluid prose and choice of words often exquisite, the writing as seductive as his personality: 'It is as though he were constantly aware of the emotional weighting that different words have, and he frames his sentences in such a way that the feelings are touched' (2011: 92). The literary masterpieces which constitute each composition—letter, sermon, or treatise—show the writer to be compassionate, conciliatory, and charitable, not prone to debate or dissention but devoutly ready to deal with the difficult decisions in death and in life.

By way of concluding this section on desire and intimacy, a passage from the *Life of Malachy* will highlight the stylistic features of a literary art in Bernard which accentuates the exuberance in living out a vision for God in fellowship with others.

Life of Malachy

Bernard's magnetism at work over a relatively short space of time may be seen in a tribute paid to a new friend, both in the lines sparkling with poetic imagination and in the zest and affection with which he holds the deceased. Here is the outworking of grace in a friendship given and received which is unhindered by nationality or rank, gathered up in a common vision for spiritual renewal: Malachy, an Irishman and Archbishop of Armagh (d. 1148) and Bernard, a Frenchman and abbot.

Bernard first met Malachy in c.1139 when the Irishman made a detour to visit Clairvaux on his way to Rome. The visit had an irreversible impact on the churchman, so much so that when his request to join Clairvaux was denied him by the pope, he left some of his companions behind him in his stead when he returned to his duties in Ireland (Holdsworth, 2011: 193–194; Matarasso, 1993: 59).

Bernard's account shows that coming to Clairvaux is a homecoming for Malachy—in more ways than one, as the visit in 1148 was to be his last. He spends his final days before his death in the company of the brothers who love and admire him. Bernard's moving account of his friend's last visit is punctuated by sorrow and joy: sorrow for the passing of a good friend and leader, but joy in the knowledge that eternal bliss awaits him. Note the way in which Bernard's flowing style incorporates scripture with effortless ease so that biblical text is often interwoven with his own graceful prose as he welcomes his friend:

> Malachy was received by us, although he came from the west, like the day star from on high visiting us in its dawning [Luke 1:78]. Ah! How the radiance of that sun filled our house with added glory! How joyful the feast-day that dawned on us at his coming! What gladness, what rejoicing in this, the day which the Lord gave! [Psa. 118:24]. As for me, trembling and weak though I was, with what swift, springing strides I ran to meet him! How happily I rushed to kiss him! With what blithe arms I hugged this grace sent to me from above! With what an eager face and spirit, my father, I brought you into my mother's house and into the chamber of her who conceived me! [Song of Songs 3:4]. What festive days I spent with you, but oh, how few! (LM, trans. Matarasso, 1993: 60)

Having touched briefly on the question of Bernard's search for friendship, one or two salient features emerge, which are of note for a twenty-first century reader. There is the sense that Bernard is a humane man who is in touch with his inner self and unafraid of laying bare his soul to friends. There is an impression of a strong personality compliant under the restraining hand of God. There is an intuition that here is a giant of a man, a leader of men, an influencer, but a complex figure. An arc drawn from this self-aware abbot to our own day shows that the fragility of relationship in a medieval world is not dissimilar to contemporary experience.

These findings are an incentive to take soundings of Bernard's depth in friendship. An in-depth probe which plummets his inner world will seek to draw out his enjoyment of male friends without a glimmer of homosexual attraction, what might be called 'gender affectivity', the absence of which does not preclude the potentiality that Bernard was physically attracted to other men (McGuire, 2020: 4). The language used in the passages examined tellingly describe the affections, which must, however, be purified and chastened within the monastic rhythm of meditation upon scripture (Pranger, 2011: 242). Before venturing to the texts themselves we must get to grips with the kind of language employed to express affection.

Affectus

The way in which loving devotions are transcribed is through a word used repeatedly viz. *affectus*. a Latin word without modern parallel, but loosely interpreted as 'a deep-seated attachment' uniting intellect and feeling (McGuire, 2020: 5). In Bernard the faculty of *affectus* functions in human attachment i.e. emotion and feeling, but also in passion which is not regarded as evil (Sommerfeldt, 2011: 372). *Affectus* is the motivation for a man to leave familiar surroundings and cleave to a new community in bonds of brotherly attachment, dependence, and loyalty; or the disposition of an attachment to a beloved person or object (McGuire, 2020: 5, 125). These ties of affection with men are written on occasion in effusive, affective language. For example, Peter Abbot of Cluny, his 'intimate friend', receives an apology from Bernard for cooling off: 'If I had perhaps grown cold towards you, as you reproach me for having done, there is no doubt that cherished by your love I shall soon grow warm again' (Le 305.1: 375).

On another level, the communication of this *affectus* is present in speech about God as a principal goal: Bernard wishes to arouse in his monks devotion to prayer and contemplation (Casey, 2011: 93). Bernard's sermons on the erotic Old Testament poem the Song of Songs do not shy away from sexual language but translate the physical union between man and woman into the passionate love of Christ for each person. Union with Christ brings about a 'marrying' or 'wedding' of the soul to the Word (SS 83.2.3, vol. 4: 182).

BERNARD'S DEPTH IN FRIENDSHIP

Jean Leclercq, the distinguished monastic scholar, states categorically that there is no evidence to suggest that Bernard's sermons on the Song of Songs were written down during, or even after, delivery. He would have spoken simply and with familiarity to his monks in the chapter house. His spontaneity in an informal setting—a kind of trial run—would in no way restrict his freedom when he composed, in written form on wax tablets, the same sermon for the public (SS, 1976, 2: xxii–xxiii). At the time of constructing the sermon Bernard would have conformed to the rule of the genre: 'He pretended to have an audience in front of him and imagined their reactions to what he said, although, of course, he was speaking only in the presence of a scribe.' The scribe would have written down, edited, and made the sermon(s) public (Leclercq, 1987: 28).

A principle of weighting words on a scale of measuring facts and feelings can be seen very clearly in Bernard's language of lament for Gerard, his beloved brother, in a piece which forms part of a sermon on the Song of Songs (SS 26.2.3.–8.14 trans. Walsh, 1976, 2: 60–73). In operation in this text are the two levels of affection discussed above viz. attachment to one another and attachment to God. Their overlapping function and the extent to which both are significant in different ways has to do with the perspective in which the passage is viewed. These ideas will be dealt with in the course of the textual analysis.

THE LANGUAGE OF LAMENT

With these comments in mind, let us turn to Bernard himself, for whom the teasing out of the right word, the most logical phrase, or the more excellent form of rhetoric is integral to the pursuit of truth. The beautiful mind conjures up beautiful truth in a strenuous effort to convey meaning: 'words spring to mind, but just the word one wants escapes one; [when] literary effect, sense, and how to convey a meaning clearly, and what should be said, and in what order it should be said, has to be carefully considered' (Le 92.1: 137–138).

The literary mechanism at work in the eulogy for Gerard is either a brilliant piece of theatrical rhetoric, designed to inspire monks to greater fervour (*affectus*) for God (Pranger, 2011: 242) or it is an authentic personal grief which grows into a generalisation about human affection (McGuire, 2020: 125). These two opposing views are not easy to reconcile. On the one hand, the constraints of the monastic life are a barrier or limitation to an indulgence or wallowing in grief; on the other, modern psychological theory encourages emotion, to let it all out. Retrospectively, an arc back to Bernard's time can impose, unfairly, a grid for grief which is not authentic because it was not the monastic custom to go public with grief. And yet Bernard does. What are we to make of this? Is the sermon a literary technique to show his monks how not to grieve? Is the sermon designed to inspire the monks to move beyond grief to God?

It is the contention of this section to choose a middle way and to agree with Leclercq that Bernard's entire doctrine is 'an intense personal experience of the interior struggle' on which he reflected daily, recognizing that it is the experience common to all (1987: 35–36). What Bernard experiences in his own life he uses as a teaching tool to confront sin and to challenge and motivate his listeners or his readership. He is not a man in upsetting emotional turmoil; that is a twenty-first century view superimposed upon a monastic context. He is a leader of men, an exemplar, an abbot compelled to communicate a way to a greater affection for God and ready to show his very human emotions as a means to to that end. This is not to say that his feelings are not genuine. Bernard's grief is real and his pain tangible. What he does with sorrow is a key to unlocking the gate to his spiritual path with others.

Song of Songs Sermon 26

Bernard was 48 at the time the sermon was delivered in 1138 (SS 26 n.17, 1976: 60). It is a homily on a single verse: 'Daughters of Jerusalem, I am dark and lovely, like the tents of Kedar or the tent curtains of Shalmah [Solomon]' (SS 26 1.1: 58). A comparison is made between the tents of Kedar and the mortal body, which is a 'soldier's tent' or a 'traveller's hut' (1.1: 59), a place of sojourn *in via*. The tent itself is black and symbolic of the darkness of fleshly sin which clings for the duration of the earthly life but will one day be cast off forever as the sojourner passes through the 'tent curtains of Solomon.' In contrast, these tents are beautiful and glorious beyond description, but Bernard cannot bring himself to address this eternal topic as 'the sorrow that oppresses me since my bereavement compels me to come to an end' (1.2: 60). The very darkness of which he has spoken so eloquently seems to overshadow the preacher.

At this precise moment there appears to be a homiletic technique whereby the *persona* of the speaker identifies with an aspect of the passage in some way (cf. Pranger, 2011: 233–237). It is as though Bernard has inserted himself into the text by arriving at the point of Gerard's exodus through the tents of Solomon into an indefinable glory. He must stop right there at the entrance to eternal bliss and lament his brother departed to that greater life. He must forego the pretence and reveal the secret fire of the sadness consuming his heart (1.2.2: 60). In the enclosed, safe space of a sermon, Bernard offloads the 'Overpowering sorrow [which] distracts my mind... drains my spirit dry.' (2.3: 60). The demise of his brother is a total eclipse of his shining star, his guide, and his friend. When Gerard went 'my heart departed from me too.' (2.3: 60).

Why had he not wept prior to the declarations now being made? Bernard's detachment from grief in the midst of the sorrowing monks is to show that his faith in God is stronger than his 'affection' (*affectus*), hence his 'dry eyes' in the wake of the bier and at the graveside, the performance of the rituals of prayer as priest—casting clay over the body of the beloved brother. He wept not while the brothers' eyes were filled with tears (2.3: 60). But now as their abbot he will show both his grief and the painful restraint he suffers as an example to them:

> Who would not be moved, even with iron for a heart, at seeing me there living on without my Gerard. All had experienced the

> loss, but regarded it as nothing in comparison with mine. And
> I? With all the force of faith that I could muster I resisted my
> feelings, striving, against my will, not to be vainly upset by what
> is but our natural destiny… Since then all the time I have forced
> myself to refrain from much weeping, though inwardly much
> troubled and sad. I could control my tears but could not control
> my sadness; in the Scripture's words: 'I was troubled and did not
> speak' [Psa.77:4]. But the sorrow that I suppressed struck deeper
> roots within, growing all the more bitter I realized, because it
> found no outlet. I confess, I am beaten. All that I endure within
> must needs issue forth. But let it be poured out before the eyes of
> my sons, who, knowing my misfortune, will look with kindness
> on my mourning and afford more sweet sympathy. (2.3: 61)

Having carefully opened the 'galling' wound of his sorrowful heart to his monks, Bernard begins to paint a picture of the attachments, the affections both natural and spiritual, which had bound him to Gerard, imploring his listeners to share in his mourning (2.4: 61–62). Gerard was a brother by blood, but bound more intimately by religious profession. Attentive to his every need and necessary for the well-being of both abbot and abbey, he strengthened Bernard's resolve, spurred him on when flagging to the study of divine things, cared for his health, and reminded him of tasks incomplete. Bernard's desolate cry, his agony directed at God but, almost as a cathartic release of feeling, breaking over his fellow monks:

> Why has he been torn from me? Why snatched from my
> embraces, a man of one mind with me, a man according to
> my heart? We loved each other in life: how can it be that death
> separates us?… How much better for me then, O Gerard, if
> I had lost my life rather than your company… Why, I ask,
> have we loved, why have we lost each other? (2.4: 61–62)

Of course there can be no answer to these rhetorical queries, but Bernard ploughs on inexorably and, rather presumptuously it feels, informs his monks that, although they have lost loved ones, they have found others more lovable. He, on the other hand, has lost his only 'consolation', his only 'comfort': 'anger has swept over me, rage is fastened on me' (3.4: 62). Metaphorically turning away from the 'congregation', he talks to Gerard, addressing him as though present:

> How I long to know what you now think about me, once so uniquely yours... Perhaps you still give thought to our miseries, now that you have plunged into the abyss of light, become engulfed in that sea of endless happiness. (3.5: 63)

Thinking through the afterlife and whether the dead still feel as they did on earth, elicits from Bernard a conclusion which must have been closely worked upon with respect to the words chosen, evoking as it does an extraordinary measure of comfort for those left behind. Earthly love is caught up into God and their remarkable twinning of souls will be remembered forever. Because Gerard has entered the power of the Lord, he has become one spirit with him, 'his whole being somehow changed into a movement of divine love.' Because God is love, 'the deeper one's union with God, the more full one is of love.' (3.5: 63). And then, a triumphant proclamation of the eternal nature of friendship:

> Your love has not been diminished but only changed; when you were clothed with God you did not divest yourself of concern for us, for God is certainly concerned about us. All that smacks of weakness you have cast away, but not what pertains to love. And since love never comes to an end, you will not forget me for ever. (3.5: 63)

Having reassured himself, and his hearers, of the bonds of friendship beyond death, Bernard recounts the many blessings his Gerard generated for him, benefits which will be tabulated at the end of this section as an evaluation of monastic attachments.

As we pursue the dramatic method implicit in this sermon, we reach the penultimate ploy or device used by the preacher viz. the use of soliloquy. Bernard seems, as it were, to hold the stage and, momentarily, to be oblivious to an audience as he ponders poetically his own death caused by the death of his friend:

> Flow on, flow on, my tears, so long on the point of brimming over; flow on, for he who dammed up your exit is here no longer. Let the flood-gates of my wretched head be opened, let my tears gush forth like fountains, that they may perchance wash away the stains of those sins that drew God's anger upon me. (5.8: 67)

With transparent honesty Bernard questions his tears, the expression of his affections, his 'emotional outburst' which is akin to that of worldly people, and yet, he argues, has a different intention. Clearly Bernard's love is on another plane!

> I am that unhappy portion prostrate in the mud, mutilated by the loss of its nobler part... My very heart is torn from me... Gerard was mine, so utterly mine... a brother to me by blood, a son by religious profession, a father by his solicitude, my comrade on the spiritual highway, my bosom friend in love... the wound is deep. (6.9: 68–69)

Bernard makes no apology for his human affections which are carnal, full of yearning and longing:

> It is but human and necessary that we respond to our friends with feeling: that we be happy in their company, disappointed in their absence. Social intercourse, especially between friends, cannot be purposeless; the reluctance to part and the yearning for each other when separated, indicate how meaningful their mutual love must be when they are together... My deepest wound is in the ardour of my love for you. (6.10: 69; 8.12: 72)

With compassion Bernard states that 'our weeping is not a sign of a lack of faith, it indicates the human condition' (8.13: 72). He recognises that he is not set apart from his monks but one with them in a common *affectus*. However, it is incumbent upon his spiritual leadership that Bernard does not allow grief to dominate the monastic rhythm, to overpower and remove them from their duties to pray and contemplate God. He must return them to the state to which they are obligated by reason of their vows: tears of compunction for sin, works of mercy for others, and hard work with the hands. He must close the sermon with a reminder of the limits and boundaries of emotion which must take its place in surrender to God, who must 'impose a limit' on his tears (cf. Pranger, 2011: 243). Here is the final piece of drama, of theatre in the chapter house, as Bernard the preacher brings his audience back to the present:

> I am ashamed of these sobs of grief that go to prove my
> unfaithfulness… You entrusted Gerard to us, you have
> claimed him back; you have but taken what was yours.
> These tears prevent me speaking further; impose a limit
> on them O Lord, bring them to an end.' (8.14: 73)

Song of Songs Sermon 27
No more excessive grief; the monastic pattern must be restored. The interruption is over; it is time for the monks to return to their meditation upon the Song of Songs. Thus, Bernard takes up once more the teaching mantle in the successive sermon:

> My brothers, our friend has gone back to his homeland, we
> have paid the full tribute of human affection to his memory, so
> I take up again the instruction which I then discontinued. As
> he is now in the state of happiness it is improper to prolong our
> mourning for him, it is out of place to appear in tears before a
> man enjoying a banquet.' (27.1. trans. Walsh, 1976, 2: 74)

We may rightly ask: was there something more than a normal affection between friends in the relationship between Bernard and his brother? The answer is not at all sinister, as though there are undertones of untoward brotherly misbehaviour. There is no evidence to suggest that the siblings were anything but extraordinarily compatible and easy with one another. What is clear from the sermon and extant literature (e.g. VP 6.27, trans. Matarasso, 1993: 27), is that Bernard relied heavily upon Gerard for a variety of reasons, not least of all for his array of skills and affections; in emergencies, in wise counsel, in burden-bearing, in rescue from danger (SS 26. 3.6: 64). Here is the one who sticks through thick and thin, the one who holds the abbot accountable as a leader.

Clearly, Gerard was Bernard's right-hand man, relieving him of many of the temporalities of abbey management and freeing him for the task of contemplation and teaching. Gerard was out there in the gardens, fields, watering systems as he supervised masons, smiths, shoemakers, weavers, and farmers (SS 3.6: 65). Gerard is more than a leisure friend, someone with whom to enjoy and share one's life; he was a necessary operator for the work of the monastery. He was an administrator, a diplomatic presence among the visitors and a go-between for the monks and their abbot.

In summary, in these words of gratitude the benefit brought by Gerard is made plain: the part their friendship had played in helping to discipline and improve the soul of Bernard, in moving him to a deeper affection for God, which in turn affects the souls and affections of others:

> *I must repeat that through you, my dear brother, I enjoyed*
> *a peaceful mind and a welcome peace; my preaching*
> *was more effective, my prayer more fruitful, my study*
> *more regular, my love more fervent.* (SS 26.3.7: 66)

The arc of friendship, which has been drawn from Bernard to his brother Gerard, has attempted to demonstrate in a particular context i.e. an abbey sermon, the depth of feeling expressed for a dear and beloved friend. Here is another example—like that of William of Thierry—of Bernard's ease when it comes to matters of the heart. These heartfelt renditions in sermon and letter are not, however, soppy, or puerile. On the contrary, the masterful skill with which Bernard develops his themes shows a wordsmith whose purpose it is to craft in every line, every word, every allusion, or biblical text, a message whose precision will impact, challenge, help and change the recipient(s). The fact that these words continue to sound out and resonate 900 years later, must surely indicate to us not only the depth of the soundings taken, but also their limpid clarity. It is as though the deeper the waters of murky human affection, the clearer everything becomes. The plunge into an ocean of grief plummeting down, down, down, until one is standing on the seabed in a translucent light on the unshakeable rock of God on which friendship is grounded and the affections stabilised.

To advance our thinking as we orbit the parameters of Bernardine influence, we consider the breadth of the spectrum which is the arc of his friendship. In order to view these relations correctly, it is necessary to understand the convention of letter-writing in the Middle Ages, as this is the primary medium in the following texts.

Epistola

The letter (*epistola*) as an art form can be said to have reached its zenith in the eleventh and twelfth centuries. The method of communication in epistolary form is a closed book to an audience reared on the occasional Christmas, bereavement, or business letter, for example, and whose default correspondence is usually an e-mail or text message. Once the why, the wherefore, and the who of medieval letter writing are decoded, the letters in Bernard's corpus become more readily understood and appreciated.

In her new introduction to Bruno Scott James's 1998 edition of his translations of Bernard's letters, Beverly Mayne Kienzle (viii) simplifies the constituent parts of a letter: salutation; securing of good will; narration; petition; conclusion. These elements were tabulated in guides for correct style in letter-writing, manuals known as *artes dictaminis*—the rules Bernard would have known well and used to his advantage. A letter could be a substitute for a sermon, or for conversation in the absence of the presence of a person, often overflowing with scripture. Kienzle (ix–x) details the scope, and function of monastic correspondence: linking distant monasteries; messages of wisdom, advice, or encouragement; business affairs or matters of doctrine; use of special messengers by people in high positions; the seal of the sender for authentication; a regular courier service circulating communities to announce deaths; reading aloud the letter to the community; a general letter handed from monk to monk for silent perusal; influential letters making the rounds of church congregations.

In the introduction to his translated volume of letters, James presents Bernard as no 'plaster saint' but as someone who, like us, experienced what it was to contend with 'ill-health, moods of depression, irritation with fools, awkward situations, and the petty persecutions of mean men with narrow horizons' (1998: xxiii). He contests the idea that Bernard was economical with words and argues that, at times, his meaning is obscured by verbose and obtuse language. This is especially true of his constant citation of biblical passages, a fashionable habit but nonetheless tedious to the point of obscuring the sense of the message (xxv). Casey (2011: 88–89), on the other hand, praises Bernard's biblical style, his ever-flowing fluency, his writing saturated with unannotated biblical text learned and memorised through perpetual meditation.

One final point must be made in preparation to beginning to read extracts from letters which show the breadth of Bernard's friendships. He is a Cistercian monk but one whose allegiance is to the *Rule of Benedict* (c.540). As such he must follow the Rule and not deviate from it. And the Rule stated:

> *A monk should on no account be allowed to receive letters, gifts, or any little tokens from his parents or from anyone else [or from his brethren], or to send them in return without the abbot's permission.* (RB 54, trans. White, 2008: 80)

Kienzle (1998: ix) does not make clear her primary source when she adds the words 'or from his brethren' to Rule 54 but alleges that Benedict anticipated problems among monks: 'The reference to letters exchanged among the brothers implies that, in the silence of the monastery, letters between members of the same community sometimes provided a means of communication.' The intermediary duty of the abbot to inscribe a boundary for his monks did not, of course, apply to Bernard who, in a position of high rank, wrote freely to whomsoever he willed, but within the constraints of the letter-writing conventions described.

BERNARD'S BREADTH OF FRIENDSHIP

Bernard's star rose with rapidity and the Abbot of Clairvaux was in great demand outside the confines of his own abbey. Elder (2011: 118-119) surmises that, quite possibly, William of Saint Thierry had a point, that Bernard's love did not, in fact, match his own. That Bernard's meteoric rise to public influencer—confidant and counsellor of popes and princes, lowly and poor—precluded the maintenance of old friends. It could be argued that Bernard's overabundant salutations of affection in his letters were simply characteristic of his age, nothing more, and do not represent genuine relationship. The question must be put whether Bernard, like Augustine, who could not manage life without friends, settled for friends whom he used for his purposes, sacrificing depth for breadth. The following texts seek to demonstrate that, despite these conflicting opinions, Bernard can almost certainly be relied upon to share something of himself in his interactions, sentiments which were, if not entirely devoid of ulterior motives at times, tender and loving—as befits true friendship.

FRIENDSHIP WITH WOMEN

Bernard was not hostile to women but his natural brothers, and his brothers in community were the foci of his friendships. The reason for this concentration may be found in the literature—the well-known stories of his temptations by women inferring that he was heterosexual in his orientation—compounded by his own assertion that a man cannot be alone with a woman for very long before sexual intercourse occurs. (McGuire, 2020: 4).

Therefore, the few letters to women which contain declarations of human affection are a rarity and quite telling in their transparency. Perhaps if Bernard had lived in a later age, more accepting of gender equality and diversity, he would have been very popular with the female sex.

Leclercq calculated that of approximately 500 letters in the collection preserved only 23 are to women (cited in McGuire, 2020: 167). It would be tempting to critique Bernard on this fact purely from a postmodern advantage and its hawk eye on inclusivity. This would certainly not be a fair or justified attack. Bernard is a product of an age when women were not central to the machinations of society. Even so, as will be seen in Chapter 3, he often saw the benefit of women's patronage for the mission of God. There is evidence to suggest, too, that he was no respecter of persons when it came to acts of charity, healing, or prayer. The Vita prima recounts how a woman of Châtillon came to Clairvaux and, falling at Bernard's feet, presented him with an offering of twelve livres, imploring the help of his prayers for her husband who was gravely ill. 'He spoke to her briefly and sent her away, saying: "Go, you will find your husband well." And so she did when she got home' (VP 1.6.27: 27)

Sommerfeldt maintains that, for Bernard, friendship can be extended to the opposite sex as it is the Spirit of God who fills his heart with love for a person or persons, be they male or female (1991: 110–111). An elaboration of this point 20 years on finds Sommerfeldt in expansive tenor. It is Bernard's psychological perspective on human nature that it pursues and finds happiness only in social togetherness, i.e. the Church, which gives him the vision that all the people of God are on a pilgrimage to union with God. It is the very diversity of the pilgrims, be they monks, clergy, or lay folk, which is the sign of unity (2011: 372).

As we trace a Bernardine arc of friendship through a selection of letters (alerted to the formal style of letter-writing discussed above), we discover that it is the vocational aspect of the journey to union with God which, for the Abbot of Clairvaux, is utterly compelling. To assist, encourage and walk beside a wayfarer desirous of attaining God—now that is a cause worthy of an investment in friendship, be they male or female.

Letter 119

Ermengarde, wife of Count Alan and a great benefactress of Clairvaux, had begun a building project of a new Cistercian abbey and had finally completed it after many ups and downs, as well as the timely intervention of Bernard. Her comings and goings in religious life mirror the fickleness of her building work, until she is persuaded by an abbot of her divine purpose. When Bernard writes, it is to Ermengarde the nun. He appears to fit our modern-day equivalent of a spiritual director in encouraging a vocation. The 'salutation' signifies their 'holy love' in Christ at this point of her life:

> To his beloved daughter in Christ, once a distinguished countess, but now a humble handmaid of Christ, the respectful affection of a holy love, from Bernard, Abbot of Clairvaux. (Le 119: 181)

The opening remark, the epistolary convention of the 'securing of good will', is Bernard's reminder that it is the work of the Holy Spirit (the term 'finger of God' is often used of the Third Person of the Trinity in medieval theology cf. Exod. 8:19 and Luke 11:20) to instil affection into his heart. It is only this action that enables Bernard to write as feelingly as he does:

> I wish I could find words to express what I feel towards you! If you could but read in my heart how great an affection for you the finger of God has there inscribed, then you would surely see how no tongue could express and no pen describe what the Spirit of God has been able to inscribe there. (181)

Bernard's development of his theme of affection forms the 'narration' aspect of the letter. He wishes to impress upon Ermengarde that, although separated by distance (monastic etiquette not permitting casual meetings between monks and nuns), she will find him present to her in spirit. (The absent in body present in spirit motif is common in Christian mysticism, cf. 1 Cor. 5:3). Beyond this, if she searches her heart, she will find that his love surpasses her own. Of course his love is greater! This is Bernard, for whom love is life's drumbeat, his *raison d'être*:

> *Absent from you in body, I am always present to you in spirit and, although neither of us can come to the other, yet you have it within your power, not yet indeed to know me, but at any rate to guess something of what I feel. Do not ever suppose that your affection for me is greater than mine for you, and so believe yourself superior to me inasmuch as you think your love surpasses mine. Search your heart and you will find mine there too and ascribe to me at least as great an affection for you as you find there for me.* (181)

The note of 'petition' just so happens to be omitted, or at least subtly disguised; there is no request from Bernard, nor query answered. The purpose of the missive is extraordinary: as her 'spiritual counsellor' who has been 'moved' by God with a 'like feeling of affectionate concern', Ermengarde is prevailed upon (petitioned) 'to see that you have me always by you.' For his part, Bernard confesses, 'I am never without you and never leave you' (181).

The conclusion to the letter is brief and to the point. Interestingly, James veers toward a dynamic translation which brings out Bernard's travelling schedule lightly dusted with what may be described as a small frisson of delight. Perhaps the kind of language used between courting couples absent from one another, the sense of being apart and having to rely on letters (text messages, e-mails).

> *I wanted to scribble these few brief lines to you from the road while travelling, and I hope, if God wills, to write to you more fully when I have the leisure.'* (181–182)

James (n.1: 182) has an italic to remark the change which his translation from the Latin brings when compared with a more prosaic rendering: 'I was anxious to write this short note to you *about my journey* while on the way.' As we come to the end of a letter made remarkable by its utter inattentiveness to practical matters, we can probably go so far as to say that here we have an example of a spiritual friendship between a man and woman, finding expression in terms of endearment born of ordinary human love.

Letter 120

The only other letter to Ermengarde is similarly without definite purpose, save that of responding to news he has had of the peace his friend experiences—presumably in a letter from her. These tidings have gladdened his heart. He is delighted that her joyfulness, which can only be of the Holy Spirit, has replaced the consolations of son, brother or home. As her spiritual advisor, Bernard is pleased that his daughter in faith has at last given birth to 'the spirit of salvation, and love' (182). But he does want to visit (an official meeting for the purposes of spiritual direction) and he is at pains to tell her this, using a topos or commonplace of letters of friendship viz. the importance to friends that they see one another (McGuire, 2020: 268):

> *How much sooner would I converse with you in your presence than write to you in your absence! Believe me, I became angry with the affairs by which I always seem to be hindered from seeing you, and I greet with joy the opportunities of seeing you which I seem to get so seldom. Such opportunities are rarely given, but I confess that their very rarity is dear to me, for it were better to see you even if occasionally than never at all. I offer you a foretaste of joy which will soon be satisfied for I hope to come to you quite soon.* (182)

Here are examples of Bernard's vivid and colourful turn of phrases. James comments that 'He is at his best when he is angry. Then words flow from his pen like thunderbolts and their effect, even at this distance of time, is very striking and moving' (1998: xxv). In his communications with Ermengarde Bernard wears his heart on his sleeve which is not replicated in quite the same way with any other nun or woman of nobility. Clearly, the ex-countess has a special place in his affections.

Letter 125

And yet there are those who profess just such a 'special' bond with Bernard. To another highborn lady, the Duchess of Burgundy, who has *not* become a nun, Bernard summons the wit to convey, almost with tongue in cheek, his expression of good will:

> *The special friendship which your Highness is supposed to have for me, a poor man, has now grown to such a pitch that whoever thinks he has offended you believes that the surest way back to your favour is through me.* (Le 125: 184)

On the basis of this 'special friendship', which seems to be public knowledge, Bernard has been petitioned by another powerful member of the gentry. He has been approached by a nobleman requesting him to intercede with many prayers and directly with the Duchess herself for the marriage of his son, a union which she opposes. Bernard's intervention is 'for the love of God and the friendship you have for me' and, true to his task, advises and warns his friend of

> *the great danger to you, if you should happen to disturb the union of two people whom it may be God's pleasure to join together.* (185)

Letter 121

On another level entirely, Bernard captures his personal response to a lady whose solicitous affections for him are a real demonstration of the kind of family he believes the Church to be. Although Beatrice, 'a noble and religious lady' is not his mother by birth, she has shown him the same sort of dutiful care that any tie of blood might demand.

In his playful play on words, 'it is no wonder that I wonder, it would only be wonderful if I were able to wonder enough', he tries to show Beatrice how she has touched him deeply by 'your many kindnesses, your frequent messages, and the innumerable and daily marks of your esteem' (182).

The use of rhetorical questions are arrows to their mark as Bernard drives home the significance of such practical concern for his well-being, which by right is in the remit of the natural family:

> My dear lady, what can I mean to you? Why are you so anxious for me?... Who of my relations and friends show the same care for me? Who ever even enquires after my health? To my friends, relations, and neighbours, 'I am discarded like a broken pitcher.' Only you never forget me. You ask after the state of my health, about the journey from which I have just returned, and the monks whom I have moved to another place. (182)

Bernard's frank appraisal of the way in which this 'mother hen', in some mysterious way, has taken the place of natural family, is unusually open for a man in his position. Once again it shows the tender warmth of a sensitive nature. Bearing in mind that Bernard had suffered the death of his mother as a teenager, his reaching out in gratitude to Beatrice is made more poignant. Perhaps the encouragement from her is a reminder to him of his dear mother who had apparently cheered him on even from the grave. William of Thierry records a period of intense struggle in the young man's life, when he was seriously considering entering a monastery, and his brothers' attempts in every which way to distract him:

> [T]hey tried their utmost to deflect his mind to literary studies and enmesh him more tightly in secular life through a love for secular learning. And, as he himself would readily admit, their delaying tactics might well have succeeded had it not been for the persistent memory of his holy mother. Again and again he fancied he saw her hurrying towards him, complaining reproachfully that he

> had not been softly nurtured for this sort of trifling, nor was it with this end in view that she had educated him. (VP 1.3.9: 21)

On another memorable occasion, which presumably an audience today would find irritating, incomprehensible, or reprehensible, Bernard uses his mother's memory to admonish his sister, Homberline, who has appeared at the monastery seeking an audience with her brother—dressed in finery. Her outward appearance is the reason for his refusal to see her and it is only her petitioning him as a humble sinner that provokes him to condescend to come out to her. He upbraids his sister, telling her to give up her worldly ways and imitate the modesty of their mother. Apparently, she listened and learned and left her husband to become a nun (VP 1.30 in McGuire, 2020: 268–269).

Following the breadth of friendship has begun to describe an arc whose curvature is brightened by the imprint of women in Bernard's life. These small vignettes depict multi-faceted relationships, perhaps a mirror of his character: somewhat whimsical, surprisingly spur-of-the-moment, warm, or rough, and uncaring. The trajectory of the arc has not bypassed family but has introduced the topic of Bernard's brothers which follows straightforwardly to his friendships with fellow monks.

FRIENDSHIP WITH MEN

Shortly after Bernard's tussle with his brothers over his monastic vocation and the mystical experience of his mother's will for him, the young man gives in to God. Riding out to join his brothers fighting in Burgundy, he turns aside into a church and there 'he prayed with a flood of tears and hands upstretched, pouring out his heart like water before the face of his Lord and God' (VP 1.3.9: 21).

Vita prima 1.3.10
William of Thierry's story might be called Gathering the Troops: the conversion of Bernard's entire family to the monastic state, commencing with a vivid metaphor of a blazing fire, which had

kindled his heart and 'first attacked his brothers, leaving only the last, too young as yet for religious life, to be a comfort to their aging father, before moving on to kinsmen, comrades, friends—wherever there was the slightest hope of conversion' (VP 1.3.10: 21). The delightful narrative weaves a pattern of familial toppling as, one by one, the dominoes fell to Bernard's charismatic faith (and visions of his mother):

> His uncle Gaudry, the Castellan of Touillon, a man of rank and reputation and renown, was the first to vote with his feet... Swift on his heels came Bartholomew, youngest but one of the brothers and not yet knighted... But Andrew, the next in age to Bernard and himself a new-made knight, found it hard to accept his brother's counsel, until suddenly he exclaimed: 'I see my mother!' And indeed she appeared to him quite distinctly, smiling serenely and approving her sons' intentions, whereupon, surrendering on the spot, another recruit left the ranks of the world for the army of Christ.' (VP 1.3.10: 21–22)

There is Guy, the oldest brother, a reflective, worldly nobleman of substance with the small problem of a noble wife. Easily overcome, reassures Bernard: either she will willingly consent to his entering the monastic life, or she will die! His wife obstinate, the good Guy does the next best thing and abandons his possessions for the hard life of a peasant, at which point, enter Bernard:

> Bernard, meanwhile, who was chasing about, rounding up this man and that, arrived on the scene, and almost at once Guy's wife fell gravely ill. Realizing how it would hurt her to kick against the goad, she begged forgiveness of Bernard, who had been sent for, and sought assent for her own entry into religion. When she and her husband had finally been parted according to ecclesiastical practice, each taking a vow of chastity, she joined a congregation of women religious, where she serves God devoutly to this day.' (VP 1.3.10: 22)

IN SEARCH OF FRIENDSHIP

What are we to make of the breakup of marriage for the sake of the monastic life? A peculiar practice indeed for a generation which appears to accept quite readily the divorce court for the sake of marrying another or living with another but would rarely separate amicably for the sake of a higher calling to God with its call to celibacy.

Gerard, the beloved brother of Bernard's eulogy and an active knight, was slower on the uptake. He dismisses the complicity of his brothers to Bernard's wishes as mere frivolity, that is, until he is wounded in battle and finds himself crying out, 'I am a monk', but is shut up prisoner nonetheless, then granted a miraculous and supernatural escape from his shackles to arrive at church ready to take his vows. Such is the art of the skilful biographer of Bernard. (VP 1.3.12: 23–24).

Fragmenta, 11

Finally, from the *Fragmenta* (VP: 24–25) the notes and jottings of Geoffrey of Auxerre, Bernard's secretary, given to William of Thierry to incorporate into his *Vita*, is the account of the contested conversion to the monastic life of one, Hugh of Vitry, a clerk of noble birth and family wealth, who just so happens to be a friend of Bernard. While the recruits in Bernard's retinue are assembled at Châtillon for six months, swelling their numbers and getting their affairs in order before taking the habit, the influential Hugh is the next in line for recruitment.

Word has got out that Bernard is going to 'Jerusalem'—the monastery of Cîteaux rather than the city—so when he turns up at Hugh's house there is an extravagantly overwhelming reaction, cited in full to illustrate the drawing power of Bernard's anointed gift for friendship, particularly when he is recruiting knights for Jesus Christ:

> [A]s soon as Hugh set eyes on him, he threw himself into his arms with tears and lamentations, but these were ignored by Bernard, who waited for Hugh to get his breath back and then disclosed

*his purpose to him. At this Hugh's grief burst out afresh and the
fountain of tears flowed yet more freely... They slept together
that night in a bed so narrow there was barely room for the two.
Even then Hugh's tears continued to flow to the point where
God's servant complained that they were keeping him awake.
When Bernard did finally fall asleep, after invoking the Holy
Spirit as was his habit, it seemed to him that he spoke to Hugh of
conversion and the power of the Lord was in his voice. (24–25)*

By morning the matter has been resolved: Hugh's tears have altered from weeping for the loss of Bernard to the service of God, to crying for his own need for conversion. Bernard is delighted with this outcome and the two friends walk and talk together arm in arm refusing to be parted. At this there is consternation among the clerks and clergy who step in to thwart the friendship:

*[T]hey tried to prize Hugh away from Bernard, fearing—
indeed they already knew—that the two were one in spirit.
They kept a tight hold on Hugh and would not allow God's
servant to speak with him on any pretext. So Bernard went
home sad, but still in his heart he trusted in the Lord. (25)*

Wiley Hugh has a secret plan to outwit his companions by rearranging his probationary twelvemonth period. On this occasion he and Bernard are seated together in synod but unable to speak due to his surly and sour protectors who hedge him in closely. Hugh is still weeping freely:

*At that moment a sudden heavy shower soaked them all and sent
them scurrying to the nearest village. But Bernard, holding Hugh
by the hand, said: 'Stay here with me in the rain.' The swift return of
fair weather found them alone in the field [where Hugh confides his
clever plan to his friend]... Hand in hand the two walked back, their
spiritual fellowship unassailably strengthened. From then on all
despaired of Hugh, and nobody even attempted to detain him. (25)*

Hugh of Vitry did indeed become a Cistercian monk and subsequently was elected Bishop of Auxerre.

The full extent of Bernard's work in extending the Cistercian Order will be examined in Chapter 3; suffice it to say that the positive impact of his life was as a moth to a candle: 'mothers hid their sons, wives their husbands, and friends their friends, lest they lose them to his persuasive charm' (Vita prima 1.14, trans. Casey, 2011: 81). The personal appeal of Bernard is singular: with astonishing simplicity of heart and commitment to his cause he swept along with him most of his immediate family, many of his extended family and countless friends. The power of his personality exerted a magnetic attraction throughout his life, not ever mere bonhomie, hail-fellow-well-met, but sincere love, good-will, supreme confidence, and courage. His zeal for the spiritual life and his love for God rushed out to meet all who came across him so that hundreds were caught in his slipstream and followed in his wake. His call was to the latent possibility in each one for a holy life, be they the lowliest of monks, highest of clerics or a stellar secular sovereign.

Extracts from the following letters to diverse men in varied circumstances, demonstrate Bernard's affectionate persuasion, his light-hearted good humour, and his no-nonsense approach to difficult situations—even as a much older man.

Letters 305 and 306

The correspondence between Peter the Venerable, Abbot of Cluny, and Bernard, Abbot of Clairvaux, is a good example of handling disputes well. Dissention over an election of a bishop and other monastic matters have left relations between these two leaders of rival orders strained. Like two battle weary elder statesmen they have circled one another. The tone in the letters is conciliatory as they seek to overcome their differences, reaching out to one another the right hand of fellowship (cf. Gal. 2:9).

Bernard is the first to move to restore the friendship, not without remonstration: his letters on two occasions have remained unanswered, which omission he raises with Peter in the manner of 'true friendship'. Nevertheless, being a spiritual man and slow to take offence he is keen to welcome the new note of 'urbanity' in his fellow abbot rather than prolong their estrangement:

> *I have only said this so as to be quite open with you and not to keep anything back from you, for this true friendship demands. Because charity believeth all things [1 Cor. 13:7], I have put away all my misgivings and am glad that you have warmed to the memory of an old friendship, and recalled a wounded friend. Being recalled I am happy to return, happy to be recalled. I have now put out of mind all grievances. Here I am, now as ever, your devoted servant, and full of gratitude for being once more your intimate friend, as you were kind enough to write. If I had perhaps grown cold towards you, as you reproach me for having done, there is no doubt that cherished by your love I shall soon grow warm again.* (305.1: 375)

Having dealt with the prickly tensions between them, Bernard reaches out to Peter with down-to-earth abbot to abbot camaraderie and tells him how things stand with his health and responsibilities:

> *I welcomed your letter with open hands. I have read it and re-read it greedily and gladly, and the more often I read it the better pleased I am. I must say I enjoy your fun. It is both pleasantly gay and seriously grave… I have decided to stay in my monastery and not go out, except once a year for the general chapter of Abbots at Cîteaux… May God be merciful and never alienate his mercy or your prayers from me. I am broken in body and have a legitimate excuse for not going about as I used to.'* (305.2: 375–376)

Peter writes back with affection, mentioning that he could not refrain from kissing Bernard's letter before reading it out to the monks. He is regretful as to the petty divisions on matters of custom which have come between the two orders and wishes magnanimously for mutual tolerance and respect (Benedictine Edition 229, in James, 1998: 376–377). In another letter he greets Bernard as 'the great and glorious pillar of the monastic Order, and indeed of the whole Church' and goes on to say that if he could choose, he would rather live with Bernard than be a king (Benedictine Edition 264, in James, 1998: 377). This is high praise from another towering personality of the twelfth century.

Struck by Peter's complete lack of malice or petulance, and his chivalrous praise, Bernard writes back with innocent joy:

> O you good man, what have you done? You have praised a sinner, you have numbered a good-for-nothing amongst the blessed!...
> Happy to be loved by you and happy in loving you. (306: 377)

Letter 307

Part of the problem, indeed nub of the matter, is that between the two orders there is some to-ing and fro-ing of monks, which Bernard addresses with respect to the monk, Galcher, who had left Cluny to join Clairvaux. Friendship in the monastic way cannot be selfish but must be for the good of all. To Peter he attempts a spiritually theological explanation, underscoring the Christian ideal of filial, that is brotherly, love, which binds the monk to both abbots who, because they honour one another, treasure him more highly. Galcher belongs to them both in a godly attachment:

> Your son Galcher has now become ours, according to those words: 'All my things are thine and thine are mine' [John 17:10]. Let him not be loved any the less for his belonging to us both; but if possible let him be loved all the more, and be all the more esteemed by me because he belongs to you and by you because he belongs to me. (378)

Sceptically, it is questionable whether such broadminded largesse is workable given the strict demarcations between the Benedictine Order of Cluny and the breakaway Cistercian Order at Clairvaux. Even their clothing is different: black-robed monks for the older order and pristine white for the fledgling habit. However, if their starting point is friendship then really, does it matter that much?

There is a biblical precedent in the appeal of Paul to Philemon—because they are friends—that Onesimus the runaway slave will be sent back 'no longer as a slave but more than a slave, a beloved brother—especially to me but how much more to you, both in the flesh and in the Lord' (Philem. 1:16).

Letter 308

There is warmth of affection in the salutation: 'To his most reverend father and dear friend Peter' and a soft intimacy and tangible relief that the contrariness between them is over. They are equal in affection but there is a hint that Bernard is skilfully underlining the equality of their status as abbots of different orders:

> Would that I were to express in this letter all that I feel towards you! Then you would certainly see clearly the love for you which God has inscribed upon my heart and engraved upon my very bones. But what need is there for me to commend myself to you in this way? For a long time now we have been united in the closest friendship, and an equal affection has rendered us equals. (378)

Letter 424

Eskil, Archbishop of Lund is a fervent admirer of Bernard and longs to join his order, a desire granted only at the end of his life. Both men have feelings of mutual affection toward one another, described by Bernard as a 'special love' which overflows into a concern for one another's worries and troubles:

> Your letter and greetings, or rather your expressions of affection, were most welcome because of the special love you and I have for each other. Your troubles are, for this reason, my own; I do not have to make them so. I cannot but grieve for your grief, dear father, or hear of your worries and troubles but with worry and trouble. Whatever provokes you touches me and wrings my heart, and whatever oppresses you weighs on me too. (493)

IN SEARCH OF FRIENDSHIP

And there is a go-between, the monk William, the messenger from Eskil delegated to bring his letter. William will act as Bernard's heart, ears, and eyes as he returns with the words from the Abbot concerning the Archbishop's vocation to the monastery. Here are the bonds of intimacy, the sharing of one heart with another by means of a trusted emissary who is party to the secrets shared:

> About that secret wish that burns in your heart, the bearer of this letter, your William, will tell you what I think; your William I say, and especially yours in the heart of Christ. Attend to what he says on this matter as you would to myself. (2:494)

Having to break off the letter for the duties of the crowds of visitors awaiting his counsel, Bernard ends hurriedly, but in no less tender style:

> But although all this may make my letter brief, it cannot lessen my affection. It can control my actions but not my heart. This is all yours to command as you wish for as long as I am alive, my very dear friend worthy of all honour and respect. (2: 494)

On the matter of the importance of a messenger there is the comical, light-hearted Letter 434 to Baldwin, Bishop of Noyon.

Letter 434
Bernard writes rather cheekily to the Bishop about the bearer of the letter, a small boy, who will eat the Bishop's bread on his arrival. Bernard counts the Bishop as a friend familiar with his carefree moralising banter when he writes that he will find out 'how mean you are from the sort of welcome you give him', but that there is not cause for worry because 'he has a small stomach and will be content with little', and that better to see him returned 'wiser rather than stouter'. Bernard's concluding remark, that the tone of the letter is his seal, shows that the Abbot is well-known for his quiet humour,

which challenges with gentle exaggeration and without intimidation (504).

Vita prima 2.5
Leaving the lofty peaks of the ecclesiastical hierarchy we come to the humdrum daily life of a monastic order. Although Bernard loved his brother-monks with an altogether 'motherly tenderness' (Saïd, 1981: 11), he could be obstinate and unyielding when it came to their physical comfort. His austerity is extreme; not all are desirous of such poverty and there is a backbench revolt from the monks of Clairvaux as they drive forward a vision for a new geographical location.

First, Bernard's attention must be drawn, not only to the workings of his own soul, but to the workaday perspectives of his monks—attentiveness given with some difficulty. There is the problem to consider, which his monks faced daily, of their Abbot's withdrawal into heavenly contemplation. How to convince their enraptured Abbot that their abbey is overcrowded and cramped? They describe their desired move to a flat area near a river with ample room for meadows, granges, shrubberies, and vineyards. Bernard resists, offering arguments against excessive wealth and labour which this project represents. It is everything his high-principled Cistercian code opposes. The brothers persist, talking him down by finding his weakness for recruitment and pointing out how wonderful prospective new monks will find such a fine place. Surely an indication of God's favour when these will be converted to join their band! Bernard is won over by their faith and common sense, good-naturedly conceding the victory of necessity over principles of poverty. (Vita prima 2.5, cited in Casey, 2011: 70-71).

For the purposes of this chapter, the arc of Bernardine friendship cannot end at a rainbow pot of a new Jerusalem in the shape of the monastic enclave at Clairvaux, but in the world outside the abbey. It is here that pieces of Bernard's letters uncover some of the inherent contradiction in his conflicted soul. He wishes other leaders to know the compromise his spiritual life suffers as he is tugged away inexorably from the cloister and into worldly matters of church and state.

Letter 326
To the Carthusian Prior of Portes Bernard offers a confidence as though in a confessional to a priest:

> It is time for me to remember myself. May my mo`nstrous life, my bitter conscience, move you to pity. I am a sort of modern chimera [a triple-bodied monster, lion, she-goat, and serpent], neither cleric nor layman. I have kept the habit of a monk, but I have long ago abandoned the life. I do not wish to tell you what I dare say you have heard from others: what I am doing, what are my purposes, through what dangers I pass in the world, or rather down what precipices I am hurled. If you have not heard, enquire and then, according to what you hear, give your advice and the support of your prayers. (4: 402)

Bernard's self-accusation of of a kind of double standard is very self-aware. He feels more part of a later century than his own at this point.

Letter 13
In mid-life (c.1130–38) Bernard addresses a letter to Prior Guy and other religious of the Grande Chartreuse. His self-deprecating manner endears this loveable man to many as he shares the storm in his soul besieged by his many trips, forays, and entanglements in the politics of Europe:

> As for me, unhappy man, naked and poor, it is my lot of labour. And unfledged nestling, I am obliged to spend most of my time out of my nest [monastery] exposed to the tempests and troubles of the world. I am shaken and upset like a drunken man, and cares devour my conscience. So once more I say have pity on me who certainly need it, even if I do not deserve it. (49)

To enter into the arc of Bernard's world of friendship is to arrive at a complex and intricate web of human connectedness. We could easily dismiss the volume and variety of written correspondence over his lifetime as negligible compared with the busy traffic on global networks, digitised online communication and archived materials today. We might think the two worlds too dissimilar to be of any practical use. However, if we are wise, we might pause and think a little more fastidiously that, even in that world of pen and ink and slow speeds of contact, it is a remarkable feat for one man to change, not only the hearts and minds of so many, but *as* a change agent to lead the many into a greater love for God by a physical relocation of their entire lives. Here are the effects of a powerful personality at work in the lives of countless others streaming into the monastic life, changing not only their minds but altering forever their way of life by his words and deeds. We find, too, that these are not one-off friendships, but ever-deepening bonds of actual accountability with monastic and non-monastic alike. We may well be intrigued as to the secret of his charisma, which is the source of his friendships and to which we must turn, the subject matter of Chapter 2.

Chapter 2

THE TRIANGULAR NATURE OF LOVE

'What do you think success is?' asked the boy.
'To love,' said the mole.

Having sampled a variety of friendships in Bernard in Chapter 1 and had a taste of his powerful, commanding, and authoritative personality (even, at times overbearing and authoritarian), we might wish to write off such a charismatic appeal as arising from sectarian Roman Catholicism. Our concern could be fuelled by worry at the breadth and depth of Bernard's relationships, which, as we shall see in Chapter 3, expand outwardly in ever increasing circles of influence from himself as an enclosed monk under vows, to a very loud voice in society. We would require good grounds for such a dismissive approach as by doing so we are eradicating an era of spirituality which was a high-water mark in Christian devotion. What we *do* require, however, are good grounds for retaining such devotional spirituality and understanding how love for God can generate friendship with others. Therefore, in this chapter, our task is to think about the source of friendship in

Bernard. Is he an especially lovable person or is there something more to it than that?

If our aim is a workable 'grid' of love, then what might that look like? For this purpose the mathematical symbol of a triangle will be used as a way of demonstrating how the love of God works and how it operates in friendship. As a theoretical notion to keep in the background of this study, the triangle will be used in two ways to develop two parts of our grid. First, the triangle represents the Trinity—Father, Son, and Holy Spirit—without which we cannot proceed and the doctrine of which must be tackled head-on. Second, the triangle is a model for joined-up relationship with God at the apex and two friends, each at the two corners of the base.

Our investigation will proceed in three parts: Bernard of Clairvaux on loving God; Aelred of Rievaulx on love and friendship; and, Aelred of Rievaulx on Christ as the third between friends. In this way the chapter will attempt first, a theological review of love and the Trinity in medieval thought and second, to encapsulate the content of these notes by way of illustration from medieval texts.

The first half of the chapter tackles the world of the Trinity and its invitation to the human soul to come up higher into an everlasting and tender embrace. Bernard's vision of adoration and union with Christ is a dynamic revival of the spirituality of love, a new breaking open of a tradition in stasis, with divine love as the bedrock of friendship.

The first part of the second half of the chapter delves deeper into the meaning of love, and charity as a mirror for the transformation of the human matrix of relationship. Aelred of Rievaulx's thoughtful and persuasive teaching is a master class on this subject. The final section of the chapter is a review of spiritual friendship in Aelred with Christ as the third Person between friends.

An investigation into Bernard on love must set him in relation to other writings of that period, an age of romantic love in which he reigned supreme. Cousins (1987: 7) declares Bernard to be the spiritual master of the path of love when other religions and secular literature were drawing on the same motif in a century which cultivated love and courtly love as a specific art in its poetry, gentle manners, and sophisticated emotions. He remarks that the cloister of the twelfth century produced a spirituality of love whose provenance and influence is not clear. Evans (1987: 5, 7) agrees that, although European love stories were the stuff of court and monastery alike, in France it was the cloister which produced a spirituality of love and that Bernard of Clairvaux became the classic guide for those who follow the path of love in Christian spirituality—supremely demonstrated in the Commedia (The Divine Comedy) which, in the 800th anniversary year of the death of its creator, seems apt for the purposes of this chapter today.

Commedia

Botterill (1994: 13–63) discusses the iconic image of Bernard in medieval culture, his superior love so ingrained in the public consciousness that the poet Dante Alighieri (1265–1321) in his epic *Commedia*, introduces Bernard at the climax of his journey to Paradise as his third and final guide to the love of God. The moment when Dante sees the white-robed elder Bernard among the celestial hosts in Paradise is described thus:

> *Around his countenance and eyes there flowed*
> *the generosity of joy, his look*
> *a gentle father's, firm and virtuous.*
> (Canto 31.161–163, trans. Kirkpatrick, 2012: 469)

Bernard tells Dante that he has been sent to help him perfectly attain his path to the eternal light of God:

> *The holy patriarch: 'So you may perfectly*
> *attain the summit of the path you take*
> *(for that I am sent, by prayer and holy love),*
> *fly through this garden with your wings of sight,*
> *for seeing this will make your gaze more fit*

to climb towards the radiance of God.'
(Canto 31.94–99: 470)

Bernard's function in the poem is to conduct Dante to God. Rooted in Catholic understanding the journey is inevitably via the Virgin Mary, whose virtue and exquisite transcendence far exceeds the gorgeous vitality of the Lady Beatrice, the darling companion of Dante on his quest for love. In the poem Mary, apart from God but as the bearer of the Son of God, is the highest form of beauty and goodness. In his writings Bernard describes her as being a house of wisdom: 'Wisdom has built a house' (Prov.9:1) and Mary is that house with the seven virtues of God as its pillars (*Sermo de Diversis* 52.1–4, trans. Dumont, 1999: 203). Bernard's devotion to Mary, whom he dearly loves, is painted in words akin to the language of romance, which indeed it is. We begin to get a glimpse of the emotional affectivity in the master of love in the following lines:

Bernardo, seeing where my eyes were set
fixed, won, attentive to her warm regard,
now turned his own so feelingly to her
that mine in wonder blazed out all the more.
(Canto 31. 139–141: 472)

But after a hymn of praise to the Virgin Mary, Bernard bids Dante look up to the ray of light which will subsume and cast away all other earthly figures in its sublime brilliance, including Bernard himself:

Now Bernard, smiling, made a sign to me
that I look up. Already, though, I was,
by my own will, as he desired I be.
My sight, becoming pure and wholly free,
entered still more then more, along the ray
of that one light which, of itself, is true.
(Canto 33.49–54: 479)

The great ray of light Dante braves as he goes forward, gathers up the universe in its love:

> Eternal light, you sojourn in yourself alone,
> Alone, you know yourself. Known to yourself,
> you, knowing, love and smile on your own being.
> (Canto 33.124–126: 481)

Here is an echo of the vision of Benedict of Nursia (c.480–c.547), who in the dead of night 'saw a light pouring down from above that dispelled all the darkness of the night… as he watched… the whole world was brought before his eyes, apparently drawn together beneath a single ray of sunlight.' (Gregory the Great, *The Second Book of the Dialogues* 200.35.3, trans. Ward, in Petersen, 1984: 216).

And finally, every longing and desire caught up into the love of God in the closing lines of the poem:

> But now my will and my desires were turned,
> as wheels that move in equilibrium,
> by love that moves the sun and other stars.
> (Canto 33.143–145: 482)

It is this 'love that moves the sun and other stars' with which we have to deal when it comes to the charism, or gift, for love which is in Bernard of Clairvaux. And for this we need to traverse the Trinity in its medieval theological setting.

BERNARD OF CLAIRVAUX ON LOVING GOD

Considering a trinitarian shape as a geometrical symbol may not sit easily with readers in the twenty-first century. However, for the medieval mind, especially those trained in the schools and universities, the precision of mathematical logic in describing the Godhead makes perfect sense. For example, $1 \times 1 \times 1 = 1$ is an excellent method of deducing the oneness of the three Persons of Father, Son, and Holy Spirit and their inseparability—the medieval doctrine of the Trinity to which Bernard subscribed. However, he disagreed with a method of logic applied to mysteries beyond logic, such as the Trinity. It is only by faith and a direct experience that we can know God (cf. Sommerfeldt, 2011: 370). Nevertheless, in order for light to dawn on Bernard's poetic rendering of God's actions in the soul, it is essential that the idea of inseparability is investigated as it pertains to the love of God.

THE LOVE IN THE TRINITY

Howard Watkin-Jones, in his great, informative tome which traces trinitarian history from the Church Fathers onwards, puts the trinitarian doctrine of inseparability in a nutshell describing the one creative energy of the three Persons as 'What One does All do.' (1922: 332). The operations of the Trinity are interdependent so that when one Person acts, all are acting simultaneously: 'The *whole* Godhead rests in *Each*, All act in the act of *Each*, no other conclusion being consistent with revelation.' (318). Bernard rested his view of the Godhead firmly on the bedrock of Augustinian thought, ideas which crept into the monasteries by way of the teachings of Gregory the Great (c.540–604) and Benedict (Casey, 2011: 94–97).

De trinitate

The following citations from Augustine's work, *De trinitate* (*On the Trinity*) demonstrate the notion of *concordia* viz. inseparability and concord—the harmony between the Three. The free-flowing movement between the Persons is of the essence of Bernard's vision of trinitarian unity as from this oneness is generated a divine energy which draws the soul to union with God.

Augustine on inseparability:

> But I do assert with absolute confidence that the Father, the Son, and the Holy Spirit, being of one and the same

> *substance, God the Creator, the omnipotent Trinity, work together inseparably.* (DeT 4.21.30, trans. McKenna: 170)

Augustine on the biblical text, 'God is love' and the inter-trinitarian relation of love between the Father, the Son, and the Holy Spirit:

> *Wherefore, if the Sacred Scripture proclaims: 'God is love,' as also that love is of God, and acts in us that we may remain in God and He in us, and we know this, because He has given us of His Spirit, then the Spirit Himself is the God who is love.* (DeT 15.19.37: 503–504)

Augustine on the Holy Spirit as the bond of love between the Father and the Son:

> *if the love whereby the Father loves the Son, and the Son the Father, reveals in an ineffable manner the union between both, what more fitting than that He, who is the Spirit, common to both, should be properly called love?* (DeT 15.19.37: 503–504)

Augustine on the work of the Spirit, who gives the self-same love between the Father and the Son to human beings, firing people with love for God and neighbour:

> He is that perfect love which joins together the Father and the Son and attaches us to them. (DeT 7.3.6: 228)

> He insinuates to us the common love by which the Father and the Son mutually love each other. (DeT 15.17.27: 491)

> When God the Holy Spirit, therefore, who proceeds from God, has been given to man, He inflames him with the love for God and his neighbour, and He Himself is love. (DeT 15.17.27–31: 491–496)

Watkin-Jones (1922 :340) expounds on the work of the Spirit: 'For this reason the Father and the Son send to men the Holy Spirit, that by His mission, which is itself a going forth of the Love of Them Both, they may become lovers of God.' He finds that drawing the soul to union with God is Bernardine piety in that the Spirit's work is to teach the soul to love. The *missio*, the mission of the Holy Spirit is in the sending and the turning of people into lovers of God (1922: 336).

We have come a little way to grasping the theological notion of trinitarian inseparability and the going forth of the love of the Father and the Son by sending the Spirit on a mission of love to the human soul. The question must now be put: Yes, but *how* does the Holy Spirit bring about the union between God and the human soul? For this question we must now engage, briefly, with the literary technique of allegory, which is key to understanding Bernard's description of the love between the soul and God.

Allegory

Allegory is a literary device and, to think allegorically, is to think and speak otherwise. In a sacred text of Scripture, for instance, allegory states a meaning which is not the obvious or literal one. A plain, matter-of-fact interpretation of a biblical passage will help us to see the context of the text and its meaning in 2-D, as it were. Allegory helps us to see, picture, or imagine with something extra, in 3-D, and can move us to the heart of reality in a way which dry doctrine cannot. Allegory begins with something insubstantial, for example, a human passion, and invents something visible to express the emotion. To access spiritual matters, we need access keys and this is where allegory finds its place. We begin, for example, with the experience of the arousal of the affections (Bernard's *affectus*) with love for God. We seek an allegorical symbol to describe this relationship. We arrive at the image or pictorial representation of bride and groom in the Song of Songs, which becomes a vehicle to depict not simply the love between a man and a woman, but the love between God and ourselves: the bridegroom is the bridegroom of every soul. The bridegroom is the bridegroom of the Church, the bride of Christ (cf. Lewis, 1958: 113, 44–48; Cousins, 1987: 10).

In the following section we track one or two figural or allegorical senses in Bernard's use of Scripture in his representation of the Spirit and Christ as Wisdom and Charity personified, i.e. given personal characteristics, in this case feminine. The technique of allegory may be seen in the way in which the Person of the Holy Spirit is shown to be at work in the soul.

The Holy Spirit teaches the soul to love

Bernard builds on the Augustinian legacy of 'affective spirituality': the desire for God located not in the intellect but in the will and which stems from a fundamental human need consummated in eternal life (Casey, 2011: 95). For Bernard the will is directed toward that which will be of benefit to the self, that which will perfect oneself. Misdirected toward the self, the will is a master of deception, directed toward God the will is humble, free, and loving.

With respect to the perfection of the will, the role of the Holy Spirit is as arbiter and discerner between the sinful, poisoned self and the purified, sweet self. The Holy Spirit is like a second skin covering the will and uniting it to God, and in this union love is birthed.

> The Holy Spirit lovingly visited the second power [the first power being reason] of the soul, the will. He found it infected with the poison of the body, but already judged by reason. He cleansed it with sweetness, making it burn with love and filling it with mercy, so that like a skin which is made pliable with oil it would stretch wide and bring the heavenly oil of love even to its enemies. And so from this second union, of the Spirit of God and the human will, love is born. (HUM 7.21, trans. Evans, 1987: 117)

However, Bernard parts company with Augustine in a significant shift and, for our purposes in this chapter, an illuminative breakaway. In analysing the functions of the soul and in place of Augustine's faculty of memory, Bernard substitutes the facility of *affectus* (examined in Chapter 1), which operates in emotion, feeling and passion, which includes the sexual attachment, as evidenced

THE TRIANGULAR NATURE OF LOVE

in the erotic love portrayed in the sermons on the Song of Songs (Sommerfeldt, 2011: 372). Bernard wants to say that God, who knows human frailty, appears in human form in the incarnation (*in carne* = in flesh, in a carnal body) to capture the affections of sinful people at an earthly level and then to draw them to a higher love in the Spirit:

> *Notice that the love of the heart is, in a certain sense, carnal, because our hearts are attracted most toward the humanity of Christ and the things he did or commanded while in the flesh… He wanted to recapture the affections of carnal men who were unable to love in any other way, by first drawing them to the salutary love of his own humanity, and then gradually to raise them to a spiritual love… Afterwards he showed them a higher degree of love when he said, 'It is the Spirit who gives life, the flesh profits nothing.'* (SS 20.6.7, trans. Walsh, 1971: 152)

Bernard teaches that the affections are turned from carnal, earthly love by an outstanding and extraordinary measure of grace moving the soul to participate in the life of the Trinity. He explains that desire for God is aroused by a threefold action of Father, Son, and Holy Spirit and he uses the image of a kiss in Sermon 8 on the Song of Songs to show this operation (SS 8.1.2, trans. Walsh, 1971: 46).

The Holy Spirit the kiss of the mouth

The bride, being the individual or the Church, asks: 'Let him kiss me with the kiss of his mouth' (Song of Songs 1:2). The kiss is the invisible breath of the favour of the Spirit as when Jesus breathed on his disciples to receive the Spirit (John 20:22). The kiss is nothing less than the gift of the Holy Spirit. The Spirit is the go-between, the concord between the Father and the Son, bringing harmony among the Three Persons and the soul. The Father is the one who kisses. The Son is the one kissed, a slightly more complicated situation, as surely the bride is the one being kissed by her bridegroom? This is indeed so, but we have here to overcome the question of the two natures in Christ: the human and the divine. Bernard achieves this union in the Son in that both natures are part of the kiss of the Holy Spirit. The divine, pre-existent Word is represented by the mouth—a good analogy of God speaking through his Son as in the Letter to the Hebrews 1:2 (SS 2.2.3, trans. Walsh, 1971: 10). But the Word became flesh, assuming or taking on human nature to come to earth and identify with, and rescue the fallen race of Adam, i.e. all of humanity. Therefore, the human nature of Jesus Christ in the bride is met by the divine nature of the mouth of the Word. This kiss of the Father, the Holy Spirit and the Word is 'fertile', not 'a mere pressing of mouth upon mouth; it is the uniting of God with man' (SS 2.2.3: 10). Through the mediator Jesus Christ, reconciling human to the divine, a new person is formed and re-created in union with God.

For Bernard, the mystical union with God in Christ—symbolised by the kiss—stirs up the affections to the adoration of the suffering Jesus (Watkin-Jones, 1922: 127). This infatuation is a total absorption, which has no truck with visions and dreams, parables, and flights of angels which weary him, 'For my Jesus utterly surpasses these in his majesty and splendour... Therefore I ask of him what I ask of neither man nor angel: that he kiss me with the kiss of his mouth.' (SS 2.1.2: 9)

The Holy Spirit the kiss of wisdom
For Bernard, the love of God is the beginning of wisdom. Wisdom is the fear of the Lord, but it is experiential, penetrating the heart through the affections and not the intellect. 'To receive the kiss of the Spirit, which is at one and the same time the spirit of wisdom and understanding (Isa.11:2), the soul should welcome it with fervour and intelligence' (Dumont 1999: 203). This is a kiss of appetites and desire as in Psalm 34:8, 'Taste and see that the Lord is good.' For this reason 'we must beg Christ, our Spouse, to give us a kiss of his mouth, as the Song says (1:2), that is, to grant us his Spirit of wisdom and intelligence: intelligence to attain and comprehend, wisdom to taste what we will have thus understood. Taste, *gustare*; this is Bernard's key word' (Fassetta, 1991, cited and trans. in Dumont, 1999: 203).

In her analysis of the Wisdom tradition as the female *Sophia*,

Barbara Newman (1990: 111), a medieval scholar, pronounces Bernard to be one of the spiritual writers at the time finding experimental ways of conceptualising the feminine divine. The common Wisdom tradition, with its images of marriage, a hen brooding over her chicks, Christ the power and wisdom of God, is understood by the medieval writers in a gender fluid form. A masculine Christ may be understood as a feminine *Sophia*. God's love affair with his people means that *Sophia* can be in either bride or groom. (Newman: 115). Bernard's image of mothering comes about because of a deep need to supplement monastic authority with affection and nurture, qualities which twelfth-century culture saw as feminine (Bynum, 1982, cited in Newman: 116). Newman makes the point that Bernard's use of the person of Charity takes over many of the functions of Wisdom—he is attempting a more awesome picture of God who is love (117).

LOVE FOR GOD

We must proceed with a Bernardine review of the response of the bride to Christ, or, to put it an a more contemporary way, how can I make space to love God above everything when there are so many demands clamouring for my devotion? The treatise *On Loving God* traces Bernard's thinking and feeling about this subject and is a development of the key concepts about love and friendship of an earlier letter to the Prior of Chartreuse (Le 12: 41–48), which was copied and placed at the end of the new treatise as integral to the work (12.34–15.39, trans. Evans, 1987: 200–205). The contents of that letter will be discussed below as part of the triangular nature of friendship in Bernard.

On Loving God

The tractate *On Loving God* (trans. Evans, 1987: 173–200) deals with the topic specified by Aimeric, a good friend of Clairvaux and cardinal deacon and chancellor of the Church of Rome. He had requested a book on loving God and Bernard obliges, with some protestation as to his unworthiness for such a task, as he is usually approached for prayers and not answers to questions (LG Prologue: 174). His opening remarks to Aimeric are succinctly pointed:

> You wish then to hear from me why and how God ought to be loved. I answer: the cause of loving God is God himself. The way to love him is without measure. Is this not enough? (LG 1.1: 174)

Clearly, there are those for whom a straightforward answer will not suffice. Bernard continues his line of argument for those who are less wise and unable to accept at face value the simple arithmetic he has declared as the reason and method for loving God:

> For two reasons, then, I say that God is to be loved for his own sake. No one can be more justly loved, or with greater benefit. Indeed, when it is asked why God ought to be loved, the question has two possible meanings. We may wonder which is the real question: whether God is to be loved because he deserves it, or because it is for our good. I give the same answer to both: There seems to me no good reason to love him which does not lie in himself. (1.1: 174)

By means of this simple synopsis, Bernard seems to imply that loving God has everything to do with God himself and nothing to do with ourselves. Later in the treatise he writes that it is beyond belief and simply incredible to him that God has first loved us—we who are insignificant human beings—with so much love and generosity (1 John 4:10). Our love back to him is to one who is not insignificant, but immense and infinite, whose greatness knows no bounds (6.16: 186).

Although Bernard tells Aimeric that we are to love God because he deserves to be loved, he also wants to make sure that Aimeric (and all those who will read his tractate) realise that there is a benefit to ourselves in loving God. There is a reward. This argument has a proviso that, although God is not loved without reward, we are not to think about a reward as the reason for loving him. For love is not a 'contract' or 'agreement'. It is freely given and it makes us spontaneous. We pursue God to love him for himself, not for the sake of something else. We do not pay someone before they have done the job!

> *True love does not ask for a reward but it deserves it. A reward is offered to him who does not yet love; it is owed to him who loves; it is given to him who perseveres… Who would think of getting someone to fence his vine or dig round his tree or build himself a house by begging him to do it, or paying him a fee? How much more does the soul that loves God ask for no reward but God? Certainly, if that is not all it asks, it does not love God.* (6.18: 187–88)

Bernard summarises his argument by stating that God is the cause of loving God and God creates the longing in us. God hopes that he will be 'so happily loved that no one will love him in vain.' God is 'our sweet hope', and he is 'riches to all who call upon him.' There is nothing better than God himself who 'gives himself as food for holy souls' (6.22:191).

The fourth order of love

The four orders, or stages of love, which had been outlined to the Prior and monks and will be discussed below in Letter 12, are recapitulated in the treatise: love of self for the sake of self; love of God for the sake of self; love of God for God's sake; love of self for the sake of God (8.23–9.30: 192–97). Of note in the replay of the exposition in the tractate is the passionate language of desire and longing given to the fourth order of love viz. love of self for the sake of God. Expanding on the inebriated lover of God for God's sake, the words become sheer poetry:

> *Dearest indeed, who are intoxicated with love. Intoxicated indeed, who deserve to be present at the wedding feast of the Lord (Rev. 19:9), eating and drinking at his table in his kingdom (Luke 22:30), when he takes his Church to him in glory, without blemish or wrinkle or any defect (Eph. 5:27). Then will he intoxicate his dearest ones*

> with the torrent of his delight (Psa. 35:9), for in the passionate
> and most chaste embrace of Bridegroom and Bride, the rush of
> the river makes glad the city of God (Psa. 45:5)… Here is fullness
> without disgust, insatiable curiosity which is not restless, an eternal
> and endless desire which knows no lack, and lastly, that sober
> intoxication (Acts 2:15) which does not come from drinking too
> much, which is no reeking of wine, but a burning for God. (11.33: 100)

Having brought his treatise almost to a close with an epiphanous vision of heaven, Bernard ends with these words:

> From this point that fourth degree of love can be possessed
> forever, when God is loved alone and above all, for now
> we do not love ourselves except for his sake; he is himself
> the reward of those who love him, the eternal reward of
> those who love him for eternity. (11.33: 199–200)

Unfortunately, for us mere mortals here on earth, the fourth order of love, the state of inebriation or intoxication seems to be reserved for heaven. It does not appear to be attainable before that heavenly bliss which awaits the saints, the Church, the Bride of Christ. This point of view is problematic. There is a sense of an unfulfilled yearning which, given the circumstances of our mortal flesh and its adhesion to the earth, is understandable. And yet, the question arises whether Bernard's helplessness in obtaining a more present union with Christ here on earth pays sufficient attention to the promise of the Holy Spirit. If the outpouring of the Holy Spirit promised in Joel 2: 28–32 is reserved only for the great day of Pentecost to get the early Church going (cf. Acts 2), then Bernard is right. The Church will live in a state of suspended longing for the Return of Christ. In this in-between stage our desire for God will never totally be fulfilled, never completely consummated. And that, too, is a right perspective.

However, there is a Pentecostal hope which gets beneath the dissatisfaction of the earthly believer to offer the gift of the Spirit, which is more than a narrow sense of a 'not yet' time. The promise

THE TRIANGULAR NATURE OF LOVE

of the Spirit is precisely to bring us nearer to God in 'now' time. We are not to be orphaned, longing for a parent, for the Spirit will be sent and will indwell and make his home in us (John 14:18) and that, declared Jesus, will bring about our oneness with God. For as he and the Father are one so shall we be drawn into a oneness with the Lord and with one another (John 17: 22–23).

LOVE FOR ONE ANOTHER

Jesus said: 'May they all be one; as you, Father, are in me, and I in you, so also may they be in us, that the world may believe that you sent me.' (John 17:21). It is to this promise that we must attend in accounting for Bernard's philosophy on God's love sent to make friends and to assist in friendship. The significance of the symbol of a triangle, which has God at the apex and friends at the corners of the base, is that a godly friendship must have as its guide the light of God right at the top. Relationship in and through God will be in and through the Spirit of God, who, as we have seen, is the harmony in the Trinity, and concord between human beings and God.

Charity in friendship

Bernard's letter to Guy, Prior of Chartreuse, together with the monks in his house begins with the salutation: 'To the most reverend of fathers and most dear of friends, Guy'. The warm affection in which Bernard holds his friend is animated by his words which have fired his heart like sparks from the fire of the Lord. In this letter we find that the close-knit friendship between them is a burning brand from God himself:

> Your burning and kindling greeting seemed to me, I confess, to have come, not from man, but from him who 'sent word to Jacob.' It was no ordinary greeting such as one gives in passing on the road, or from habit; I could feel it came from the heart, a welcome and unexpected benison. May the Lord bless you for troubling to meet me, your child, with such a blessing in your letter to me

> that you have given me the courage to write back to you, after
> I had for so long wanted to, but not dared. (Le 12.1: 41-42)

The presupposition that God has brought them into fellowship in this way is very important for understanding the way in which Bernard sees friendship. Friendship does not exist for its own sake but is part and parcel of God's greater plan. Friends are born in God and remain crucial to his divine purpose for community. And this supernatural insertion into human friendship is the compelling love of God, i.e. *caritas*, translated 'charity'. The following passage shows the outworking of a relationship of love, whereby one is drawn away from the contemplation of God to be attentive to the friend. Love tugs boldly at Guy's heart, alluring him to leave his devotions and turn towards Bernard:

> But what I do not dare, charity does. She knocks confidently
> on the door of a friend, knowing that she is the mother of
> friendships and will not be repulsed. Sweet as your leisure is,
> she does not fear to disturb it a little on her business. She it
> is who, whenever she wishes, can draw you away from your
> contemplation of God for her own sake; and it was she who,
> when she wished, made you attentive to me. (12.2: 42)

Such a divine connection in God gives rise to wonderful and amiable blessings. Bernard continues to ruminate on Guy's outstretched hand of friendship, freely given, which is an encouragement to his own spiritual growth:

> [Y]ou have not thought it at all beneath you, not only to bear
> with me when I am speaking, but moreover kindly to encourage
> me to speak when I am silent. I embrace your goodness, I admire
> your condescension, I praise and venerate the purity of your
> intention which leads you to rejoice in the Lord for what you
> consider my progress. I glory in the testimony you have given me
> of your goodwill, in your spontaneous friendliness. (12.2: 42)

There has been, however, a human agent in the divine plan of getting these two souls together, one whom Bernard praises as a 'worthy man'. The go-between described as a 'religious' is presumably a monk sent from the Prior. He performs his duties and verifies Bernard's sanctity and suitability to Guy. Thus Bernard can comment with enthusiasm and flair, not neglecting to point out that he, too, has discerned the spirit in Guy, ascertaining what manner of man he is and pleased at the pure state of his soul. Such is Bernard's confidence in Guy that he believes that they will enjoy 'an even closer and more intimate affection'. These two leaders have tested each other as to the purity of their respective spiritual states:

> [I]t will ever be for me a day of joy and a day worthy of lasting remembrance on which I was honoured to see and welcome that worthy man through whom I was received into your affections. Although it is clear from your letters that you had received me into your affections even before this, yet now I understand it will be with an even closer and more intimate affection, since he has told you certain favourable things about me which he doubtless believed, although without sufficient cause… You have listened to him, you have believed him, you have rejoiced in what he said, you have written to me, and thereby you have gladdened me not a little, not only because I have won a place and no small place in your affections, but also because you have shown me something of the purity of your own soul. In a few words you have shown me for certain of what spirit you are. (12.2: 42–43)

Clearly these two men, who are in positions of power in the Church, enjoy an intimate liaison and are not shy of expressing their affection for one another. Moreover, they are not loathe to have their heartfelt desires made known to the wider community, this letter being addressed to Guy and the 'other saints who are with them' i.e. the monks of the Order of the Grande Chartreuse, to whom the epistle will be read out loud. Given these conventions it is necessary that we understand the theological grounds for the sentiments about love (or charity) heralded by Bernard and alluded to in the section above.

The four stages of love

Having examined the intricacies of testing friendship, the letter goes on to describe the progress of love, the four orders, or stages which begin with love for the self, then love for God, after which proceeding to other goods and people. Bernard is quick to acknowledge that love starts in the flesh because we are born of the desire of the flesh; therefore, the first stage is love of self and it is carnal, or fleshly:

> At first a man loves himself for his own sake. He is
> flesh and is able only to know himself. (12.8: 46)

The second stage occurs when a man sees that God is necessary for himself, which is love for God for self's sake, for selfish reasons:

> But when he sees that he cannot subsist of himself, then
> he begins by faith to seek and love God as necessary for
> himself. And so in the second stage he loves God, not
> yet for God's sake but for his own sake. (12.8: 46)

The third stage is that state of spiritual growth whereby, little by little, there is a gradual coming to know God through prayer and obedience, and love of God for God's sake, which is completely selfless:

> However, when on account of his own necessity, he begins to
> meditate, read, pray, and obey, he becomes accustomed little by
> little to know God and consequently to delight in him. When he has
> tasted and found how sweet is the Lord he passes to the third stage
> wherein he loves God for God's sake and not for his own. (12.8: 46)

The fourth stage is love of self for God's sake and requires forgetting self. Bernard is dubious as to the possibility of ever attaining level four in this life—as we have seen—and so can only look forward to remaining in the third stage:

> And here he remains, for I doubt whether the fourth stage has ever been fully reached in this life by any man, the stage, that is, wherein a man loves himself only for God's sake. Let those say who have experienced it; I confess that to me it seems impossible. It will come about, doubtless, when the good and faithful servant shall have been brought into the joy of his Lord and become inebriated with the fulness of the house of God. For he will then be wholly lost in God as one inebriated and henceforth cleave to him as if one in spirit with him, forgetful, in a wonderful manner, of himself and, as it were, completely out of himself. (12.8: 46–47)

The secret of spiritual friendship between one monk and another is, for Bernard, to enter the spiritual powers of the Lord in a preoccupation with the love of the Spirit so that carnal needs are absent and even weak human affections are transformed into divine powers. This kind of friendship does not exist on a human carnal level. Although the friendship will begin at this first 'fleshly' stage, it must pass through it to the second stage, that which is still entirely selfish but which includes God in it. By the third stage the friendship will have reached a selfless state and exist for the sake of God. By the final stage friendship will be outside of itself and oblivious to the other as its absorption with God is complete.

AELRED OF RIEVAULX ON LOVE AND FRIENDSHIP

Before we come to any philosophical, metaphysical, abstract, theological, or spiritual idea of the nature of friendship in Aelred of Rievaulx, we must place both the writer and his writings in context. Aelred, the son of a priest from Hexham in Northumberland, educated at the cathedral school at Durham, was sent as a 14-year-old to the court of King David I of Scotland and brought up with the princes. In the next 10 years he would take on increasing responsibility travelling on David's business until 1134 when he entered the monastery of Rievaulx in Yorkshire, established by white monks sent from France by Bernard—a life for which Aelred had long yearned (Dutton, 2010: 14–15). Eight years a choir monk (a white-robed monk), then sent to Rome on a diplomatic mission, returning to Rievaulx to be appointed novice master (training new monks) for a year and then elected Abbot of Revesby in Lincolnshire. After a short tenure, the 37-year old was elected abbot of Rievaulx, a position he held for nearly 20 years until his death in 1167 (Matarasso, 1993: 149–150).

These are the plain facts of Aelred's life; a more nuanced history is narrated (not as a fable but still rather favourably, as is the wont of the hagiographer) by his biographer, Walter Daniel, a monk at Rievaulx who knew his friend well. We will draw out one or two informative insights into the character of Walter's hero, striking features which tell us something of this remarkable man's genius for friendship. We will use these distinctives as a guide to pinpoint exactly why and how Aelred was such a successful friend. This will lead us to the writings and a closer examination of the texts for which he is most famous viz. *Speculum caritatis* (*Mirror of Charity*) and *De spiritali amicitia* (*On Spiritual Friendship*).

The Life of Aelred

Of interest is the fact that Aelred's 'conversion' to the monastic life is aided and abetted by friends. There is the chance conversation, while on business to York, with Waltheof, a boyhood companion in the royal court, which opens his ears to the new Cistercian Order close by at Rievaulx of which 'he learned, by a happily timed report from a close friend' (LA 5, n.3, trans. Matarasso, 1993: 153, 312). There is the likely intervention of an influential friend, the patron of the new monastery of Rievaulx and lord of Helmsley Castle, who at the incentive of King David, took the inquirer on a visit to the abbey a few miles away. On Aelred's return journey on the road back north to Scotland, the pull proves too strong and he turns aside from his party to ride down the steep track to Rievaulx (Carmichael, 2004: 74;

Dutton, 2010: 14–15; Matarasso, 1993: 155). In this timely intersection of events we see the young man's heart open to the guidance of others as he finds his spiritual path, exchanging his service to an earthly king for the higher King.

Aelred's open-heartedness is a singular trademark of his relationships, displayed most admirably in an accompaniment he makes with a monk struggling with his vows. The issue for Aelred the novice master, as with all orders is this: to release the monk under a cloud or to accommodate him in the community in the hopes that he will come to heel (RB 28, 29: 49, 50)? A secular clerk is admitted to the novice's cell:

> *This clerk was thoroughly unstable, forever wavering between one thing and the next, and would bend now this way, now that, like a reed in the wind of his changeable will. The tender-hearted Aelred was upset by this, and in his pity for the man said to God in his heart: 'Give me this soul.'* (LA 15: 155)

The pressure builds and the moment arrives when the brother confides to Aelred his decision to renounce his vows and leave the monastery. Aelred counsels him not 'to will his own destruction' (LA 15: 156). Turning a deaf ear the wayward monk does indeed leave the outer monastic enclosure and wanders all day in the woods until he comes again to the same path on the perimeter on which he had so 'fatuously' left. Aelred must have been looking out for him, for he runs to meet him and throws his arms about him, kissing him and telling him how he has wept for his safety. Walter praises the 'man of mercy', who had not divulged the escape to the abbot for fear of his severity and reprisals which could hurt his novice, but had trusted in his 'prophet's insight' that he would benefit by returning. Walter has a satisfactory ending to his tale:

> *And so it turned out; for through the selflessness of Aelred's prayer that brother ended his life clothed in the sacred habit, in Aelred's hands.* (15: 156)

IN SEARCH OF FRIENDSHIP

This display of monkish togetherness is characteristic of Aelred and we will see its properties in the analyses of his texts on love and friendship. In the Vita prima, however, Walter wants to make it quite clear that the incident in the case of the runaway monk is no superficial flash in the pan one-off event. Aelred keeps him under his wing and when he flies off to be abbot to Revesby, the recalcitrant brother is part of that flight. During this time, he makes his complaint to Aelred about the food, the wearisome drill of prayer, the daily chores, and on and on. His abbot promises him softer clothing and all the small indulgences allowed, if only he will stay with him. When this offer is declined, Aelred goes to his cell to pray with weeping and fasting. The difficult monk begins his getaway to the gate of the enclosure and this is where he sticks. He cannot, simply cannot break out. The double doors are an unyielding iron wall. In a 'fury of frustration' he takes hold of the hinges and tries to stretch the doors to open to let him out. To no avail. The air has been turned into a barrier by the prayers of the blessed Aelred! He returns in his right mind to pledge 'future constancy' (22: 156–157). Walter's praises are sky-high:

> 'Well done, my son,' replies the saint, 'welcome back.
> God who has brought you safely home has indeed been
> merciful to me.' Let all who have a special love for Aelred
> read this miracle over and over again. (22: 157)

In Aelred we see a serious commitment to the call upon his brothers' lives but we see that his method of helping the call is friendly and accessible. He seems not to lord is over others. But he is discerning. The final episode in the saga of the ambivalent monk shows Aelred at work in hearing, and discerning God's will. In a night dream he is given a prophecy that his rebellious monk will soon die of a grave illness and better that he be in, rather than out of, the monastery. On his return from a journey on abbey business, the monk in question is met with joyful love by his abbot who tells him that he will soon be made perfect in glory! He gets the wrong end of the stick and thinks

Aelred means perpetual enclosure never to be allowed out again! He demands, therefore, that he return home for a month to live it up before this final imprisonment, but with great love Aelred coaxes him to remain: 'I can no longer live without you, nor shall you die without me.' Within six days his protégé has fallen ill. He is given sedulous care by his father abbot and dies a few days later, his head cradled in Aelred's hands (28: 157–159).

These are the traits we have found in Aelred: open-hearted friendship, persistent prayer for the weak, perseverance with the troubled, and loving spiritual guidance for the uncooperative. The words Walter Daniel uses to describe the safe harbour which is Rievaulx can only be an extension of the welcoming spirituality of its abbot trickled down to all the brothers in community:

> *This man turned Rievaulx into a veritable stronghold for the comfort and support of the weak, the fostering of the strong and sound... What man so crushed or scorned but found there a haven of quietness? Who ever came to Rievaulx crippled in spirit and did not find in Aelred a loving father, and all they needed of comfort in the brethren? When was anyone ever expelled from that house on account of physical or moral frailty, unless his wickedness was such as to offend the whole community? (29: 159)*

Aelred's community is filled with monastic rejects denied access to other houses and these 'rolling stones' came from all over, even from foreign countries to 'Rievaulx, the mother of mercy' (29: 159). Woe betide any brother who complained about inappropriate behaviour in their midst:

> *'No brother, no; do not kill the soul for which Christ died, nor drive away the glory from this house... the supreme and singular glory of Rievaulx is this: that it teaches us above all else forbearance with the weak and compassion for others in their necessities...*
> *'All,' he [Aelred] would add, 'weak and strong alike, should find in Rievaulx a place of peace... and limitless quietude of love.' (29: 159)*

Aelred's ruse of inclusivity for all the walking wounded men who stumbled into Rievaulx clearly worked. The monastery expanded exponentially during his 20 years in abbatial office so that at the time of his death there were 140 choir monks (*monachi*), 240 lay-brothers (*conversi*)—the backbone of the labour force—and 260 laymen (*mercenarii*) associated with the spiritual and material life of the abbey and complementary to the gangs of workmen on the granges (LA 29, Matarasso, 1993: 160, n.14: 313).

Aelred's Rievaulx is an echo of Augustine's brotherhood aspiring to the friendship-ideal. Intended as a 'battle-school' for the front-line of the Church, the monastic community of Hippo was also a 'hospital for some of the more striking misfits and casualties of life' (Chadwick, 1986: 58, cited in Carmichael, 2004: 73). 700 years on from Augustine, the Cistercian Order espoused this same ethos of fraternity. Its *modus operandi* did not arise from a type of kindly humanism or even a philosophical theory of Christian altruism. To the contrary, the entire theological edifice of the order was built around the spiritual notion that the grace of the Holy Spirit worked through the fellowship of the brothers in Christ as they helped one another along the path to sanctification. Here is the monastic tradition: the enabling of a fellow monk to pursue the way of holiness; and the handing down of the form proper to the monk from generation to generation (Dumont, 1990: 11). From time to time there arose monks brilliantly equipped for this task of monastic formation, standing out as luminaires, and casting their light far and wide to lasting effect. Bernard of Clairvaux and Aelred of Rievaulx are such phenomena (Dumont, 1990: 11–12).

CHARITY IN SPIRITUAL FORMATION

Mastery of a complex process of formation was not in every abbot's gift but Bernard recognises in Aelred a man of worldly experience in practical affairs, infinite charm and apparently trapped in sensuality in his former pre-monastic life. McGuire notes the scholarly controversy about the exact nature of Aelred's youthful sins but assesses Bernard's wisdom in accepting that the younger man had benefited from his experiences by integrating his learning into the Cistercian way of life. He finds in both lives a tone of homoeroticism but that Aelred's sublimation of his impulses at Rievaulx created an atmosphere of affectivity that fulfilled his own needs. He observes that there is an element of eroticism in the way in which Bernard inspired his monks to share each other's lives in spiritual intimacy (2020: 175–272).

However, it must be stated unequivocally that life's experience was not the deciding factor in the shaping of a monk. Aelred's spiritual formation in the Cistercian 'school of love' was ordered by an exceptionally tough regime: apart from a sparse diet, little sleep and much prayer, the novice had to meditate on five books of the Old Testament designed for detachment from the world, purification, and eventual mystical heights viz. Ecclesiastes for the emptiness of worldly pleasures, Proverbs and Ecclesiasticus for self-knowledge and virtue, Wisdom and the Song of Songs for a life of contemplation (SS 1.1.1–2, trans. Walsh, 1971: 1, 1–2; Carmichael, 2004: 74). The boot camp for Cistercian living was a strict asceticism, a participation in the sufferings of Jesus so that the monk learned *caritas* (love or charity).

Another word for love is *amor* i.e. the human being's natural capacity to love. When used well and ordered by God's grace, *amor* becomes *caritas*; under lust or ambition *amor* becomes *cupiditas* (yearning, desire, lust). The aim of the monastic life is to replace *cupiditas* with *caritas* (Carmichael, 2004: 75). This is the subject on which Bernard is determined Aelred will write, a treatise on love *Speculum caritatis* (*Mirror of Charity*).

A twelfth-century Latin manuscript from a Benedictine abbey in Douai tells the story of the commissioning of the treatise *Speculum caritatis* (Fig 2. France, 2011: 311). There is the image of Bernard in the top left-hand corner of the folio seated in the centre of the initial E, the opening vowel of the letter which will follow. In his hand is a scroll depicting the text of that letter and two of his fingers are raised in blessing. He is looking down upon a figure in the far right half of the opposite folio seated in the letter V, the opening initial of the treatise beneath. The image is a young, tonsured monk in a white habit identified by the words above his head: *Ailred(us) mo(nachus)* translated as 'Aelred the monk'. The treatise is *Speculum caritatis*. The letter contains Bernard's instruction to Aelred to write a treatise on love (France, 2011: 310).

The commissioning letter

Traditionally the letter (Le 177, 1998: 245–247) has been attributed to Gervase, Abbot of Louth Park, but it has been argued conclusively that the writer is Bernard and the style authoritative (James, 1998: 245-46), contra McGuire's remark that the piece is 'one genuinely beautiful letter that is a masterpiece of Cistercian spirituality' (2020: 174).

The salutation begins: 'To Aelred, Abbot of Rievaulx.' Bernard lightly ticks off Aelred for disobeying his instruction to write a treatise on charity. Bernard will not accept his abbot's excuses of illiteracy and inferior oratory, the usual convention of pleading humility and inaptitude in spiritual writers. He cajoles persuasively that these hesitations 'serve rather to inflame than extinguish the spark of my desire, because knowledge that comes from the school of the Holy Spirit rather than the schools of rhetoric will savour all the sweeter to me' (Le 177: 246–247). We recognise instantly Bernard's view held fast that true knowledge is revealed by the Spirit experientially and not through learned methods of reasoning. He sets out his hard and fast rule by means of a rather indelicate, visceral image:

> And so I think that with that maul of yours you will be able to strike something out of those rocks that you have not got by your own wits from the bookshelves of the schoolmen, and that you will have experienced sometimes under the shade of a tree during the heats of midday what you would never have learned in the schools. (247)

Bernard is pulling rank on Aelred as he orders obedience:

> I therefore order you in the name of Jesus Christ, and in the Spirit
> of our God, that you do not delay to write down those thoughts
> that have occurred to you, in your long meditations. (247)

The subject and content are set down clearly as a treatise on the excellence of charity so that all may see in what Aelred writes, as if in a mirror, the sheer sweetness of this virtue and how heavy and sorrowful without it (247).

The closing instruction employs a clever device, the modern equivalent along the lines of 'the buck stops here.' Bernard will take full responsibility for this work—the title of which he has already decided—and will achieve this by placing this letter at the start of the treatise. Everyone will then know that Aelred has submitted to Bernard and blame the leader of the Cistercian world for anything displeasing:

> But, for the sake of your modesty, let this letter be put at
> the beginning of the work, so that whatever in the Mirror
> of Charity (for that is the name I give it) should displease
> the reader shall be imputed to me who have commanded
> it and not to you who have obeyed by writing it. (247)

Speculum

We come again to the literary conceit of allegory in the use of the Latin word *speculum*. In the Church Fathers the Trinity forms a *speculum*, a 'mirror' by means of which difficult trinitarian statements in Scripture and church tradition are harmonised and made plausible for faith (Kasper, 1982: 251). *Speculum* in Gregory the Great is the transitory nature of this world as a 'mirror' through which to see into the next world (Petersen, 1984: 54). In medieval texts *speculum* is used for the reflection of divine and human objects so as to be free of distortion. For example, *Speculum historiale* (Mirror of History) and *Speculum naturale* (Mirror of Nature) by Vincent of Beauvais (Chenu, 1968: 116). In medieval texts *speculum* can show a Life-Book correspondence: meditation on the Bible and its relation to the whole of reality, and to the self, so that the text is a mirror to the self i.e. *liber et speculum*, 'text and mirror' (Ricoeur, 1981: 50–57). This last example is not the sense in which Aelred's treatise is fashioned. He makes no use of the verses in the Letter of James likening the person hearing God's word and not acting on it to one who looks intently into a mirror promptly forgetting his appearance (1:22-25). Aelred must use *speculum* 'mirror' as that which reveals the true nature of love to be *caritas* (charity, not natural love or lustful love or physical love). The mirror should show, too, how *caritas* love is revealed in behaviour. This is his commission.

Mirror of Love

The rigorous lifestyle, which is the monk's yoke, is made sweeter by love. In fact, love is the only way in which the disciplines can be endured and perfected. Herein lies the basic thesis of Aelred's work. How is this love to be attained and how may a monk be formed into love?

Formation occurs in the wrong or the right use of love, the obtaining of happiness for its fruit being the motivation for the choice made i.e. love chooses that which will give pleasure:

> Let us now make a finer distinction between right and wrong use of love. It seems to me that its use consists of three things: the choice, the development, and the fruit. The choice proceeds from reason, the development is in desire and act, and the fruit is in the object... And so each person, according either to the degree of his faith and understanding, or to illusions arising from error or to his sensory experience, puts his happiness in the fruit of one thing or another. Then, without any hesitation, he chooses for his enjoyment what he supposes capable by its fruit of making him happy. Love [amor] makes this choice... It is for love to choose what it wants for its enjoyment. (MC 3.8.22, trans. Connor, 1990: 236)

There is a triangular nature to this pattern which suits our chapter's purpose. These three things: first, the choice to love rightly. This is

THE TRIANGULAR NATURE OF LOVE

the non-negotiable fact that, by virtue of being a disciple of Jesus, the choice has already been made for the first commandment to love God (Matt.22:37) and what follows as the second law, the choice to love one's neighbour (Matt.22:39), is neither an option (3.9.27: 238).

These three things: second, the development of love, either inwardly toward desire or outwardly toward action. The question is 'what the things are which, like goads, arouse love and move it in these two directions' (3.10.29: 240). The development of love stems from one of two sources viz. reason, the rational faculty (*ratio*) or attachment (*affectus*). Which one shall we follow (3.10.30: 240)? *Affectus* or attachment is 'a kind of spontaneous, pleasant inclination of the spirit toward someone' (3.11.31: 241). However, attachment can be of six types: 'spiritual' attachment is inspired by the Holy Spirit or by the devil's meddling (3.11.31: 241); 'rational' attachment is admiration of virtue (3.12.33: 242); 'irrational' attachment is movement toward worldly people (3.12.34: 243); 'dutiful' attachment is devotion to service (3.13.35: 243–244); 'natural' attachment is toward one's own flesh and blood (3.14.36: 244–245); 'physical' attachment is attracted by elegant appearance for good or ill (3.15.38: 246–247). 'When these attachments move the spirit there is either a visitation [from God] or a temptation' (3.16.39: 247).

These three things: third, the fruit of love which gives enjoyment or pleasure in a summary of 'the whole force of love' (3.21.49: 254) which can lead toward God or away from God:

> First, if the mind chooses something for its enjoyment, then reaches out to it by a kind of inward desire, and finally does what will enable it to attain what it desires, this should without any doubt be called 'to love'. The more fervently and insistently someone carries this through, the more also does he love. If he does this out of attachment [*affectus*], he surely loves more sweetly and therefore acts with greater facility... if the choice has been perverse, so that someone selects for his enjoyment something he should not, then what follows on this choice will be perverse and the love will be perverse and should be tallied

> *under the word 'self-centredness' and not 'charity.' As we have taught above, anything that the seduced or deceived mind chooses for its enjoyment, other than God in himself or a neighbour in God, exceeds the boundaries of real love.* (3.21.49: 254–255)

There is, too, a triangular pattern to Aelred's teasing out of the attachments as being in God or not in God in the degrees of attachments. Attachment (*affectus*) can be either 'in God' or 'for God's sake' and there is a fine distinction between the two. Attachment can start by being taken on for the sake of the other and become an attachment for the sake of God because it is in God in a good way (a triangular shape). Attachment can also be for the sake of oneself and not in God nor for the sake of God (not a triangular pattern but a straight line between two persons):

> [I]f all one's love is shown someone on whom his spirit lavishes itself by some spontaneous, pleasant inclination according to attachment, that person is loved neither in God nor for God's sake, but rather for his own sake. But if the one whom that attachment encircles is also taken into a person's love of God, that love savours of attachment, but its expression is subject to the moderating control of reason. At the outset love of this person is not taken on for God's sake, but it is exercised in God in a wholesome way… that person is loved not for his own sake, but solely for God's. (3.26.62: 263–264)

Carmichael underscores the three kinds of love which are interdependent on one another: love of God, love of self and love of neighbour. This deep and intuitive threefold cord in Aelred is apparently unusual in western thought (2004: 77). This 'triple love' suits our purpose once again, of the triangular nature of love:

> [W]e must consider that although there is an evident distinction in this triple love, a marvellous bond nevertheless does exist among the three, so that each is found in all, and all in each. None of them can be possessed without all. And when one wavers they all

diminish. Someone who does not love his neighbour or God does not love himself, and someone who does not love his neighbour as himself does not love himself. Furthermore, someone who does not love his neighbour is proven not to love God. (3.2.3: 223)

If all three loves are necessary and, in a way equal, which one comes first? Aelred seems clear that 'a certain part of this love' is the prior grace which acts first in drawing us to God, thereby making all other loves possible (3.2.4: 223).

Having traced the history of love in the human-divine interaction, Aelred wants to dwell, finally on the potential of love, which is not dutiful, neighbourly, reasonable, or natural, but is simply for the enjoyment of the other. Aelred wants to break through an Augustinian barrier which made this sort of enjoyment of others possible only in eternal life, by claiming that here on earth there can be the fruit of enjoyment of one another:

> There is a temporal enjoyment [fructus i.e. fruitfulness] by which we can enjoy one another in this life, as Paul enjoyed Philemon [Philem. 20], and there is an eternal enjoyment by which we shall enjoy one another in heaven. (3.39.108: 297)

Aelred supposes that because we use different people for different purposes, some for testing, some for instruction, some for consolation, and some for sustenance, it follows that not everyone will be *enjoyed* but everyone will be shown *charity*:

> Only those whom we cherish with fond attachment, no matter which of these categories they may be in, do we use for sweetness of life and delight in spirit. These [persons] we can enjoy even at present, that is, we can use them with joy and delight... Wherefore, charity can be shown to everyone by everyone in this life... but as far as enjoyment is concerned, it can be shown to everyone only by a few, or even by no one at all. (3.39.108: 297)

IN SEARCH OF FRIENDSHIP

And now, in the final closing sections of the treatise, Aelred comes to the nub of the matter which is the springboard for the later treatise *On Spiritual Friendship*: the possibility that, in this life there may indeed be *particular* friends who share an intimate spiritual relationship:

> Moreover, it is no mean consolation in this life to have someone with whom you can be united by an intimate attachment and the embrace of very holy love, to have someone in whom your spirit may rest, to whom you can pour out your soul, to whose gracious conversation you may flee for refuge amid sadness, as to consoling songs; or to the most generous bosom of whose friendship you may approach in safety amid the many troubles of this world; to whose most loving breast you may without hesitation confide all your inmost thoughts, as to yourself; by whose spiritual kisses as by medicinal ointments you may sweat out of yourself the weariness of agitating cares. Someone who will weep with you in anxiety, rejoice with you in prosperity, seek with you in doubts, someone you can let into the secret chamber of your mind by the bonds of love, so that even when absent in body he is present in spirit... you alone may repose with him alone in the embrace of charity, the kiss of unity, with the sweetness of the Holy Spirit flowing between you. Still more, you may be so united to him and approach him so closely and so mingle your spirit with his, that the two become one. (3.39.109: 299)

And just to be clear that the above passage is rooted in a spiritual meaning, Aelred swiftly closes the door on an interpretation which could lead to the assumption that he is endorsing physical, or sexual contact, between brothers. *Caritas* is not *cupiditas*; *caritas* can never be lust, or passion; *caritas* is pure and spotless, as should be the love between brothers:

> Let anyone who finds it pleasant to enjoy his friend see to it that he enjoys him in the Lord, not in the world or in the pleasures of the flesh, but in joyfulness of spirit... all flattery and fawning

> *are checked... patting each other on the back and conniving with each other... taking care not to offend one another, they incur each other's ruin because they do not enjoy themselves in the liberty of justice or in the Lord.* (3.40.111: 299–300)

The 'mirror' shows charity between friends on a higher plane of spiritual connectedness and yet thoroughly human:

> *Let us now refresh one another by confiding our mutual secrets, now long together for the blessed vision of Jesus, and for heavenly well-being. If we relax our tense spirits with some pleasant and less lofty subjects, as is sometimes useful, let these moments of relaxation be filled with rectitude and free of frivolity.* (3.40.112: 300)

LOVE IS THE FOUNTAINHEAD OF FRIENDSHIP

As we draw the section on charity as a mirror to a close—and before we commence Aelred's thinking on Christ between friends—a short survey of Book 3 of the treatise On Spiritual Friendship (De spiritali amicitia) will help to nail down and cement the virtue and loveliness of intimate friendships as enunciated above.

The great treatise *Mirror of Charity* is unparalleled for its logical beauty and stylistic synergy. The follow-up *On Spiritual Friendship* cannot surpass but only impress again the main ideas of the former work in a series of hypothetical dialogues between Aelred and his brother monks. Book 3 has Aelred in conversation with Gratian and Walter Daniel (irascible friend and biographer)—a good triangular dialogue!

On Spiritual Friendship 3

The content of Book 3 is on the theme of the right conditions necessary to ensure that a friendship continues undisturbed. Aelred encourages Walter as they begin a discussion with Gratian: 'Gratian is a better friend of yours than you suspected.' Walter retorts somewhat irritably: 'When he is everybody's friend, how could he fail to be mine? But since we are both at hand... let's not be ungrateful for this interlude of leisure' (SF 3.1, trans. Braceland, 2010: 88). At once Aelred begins the discussion by laying a foundation for friendship:

> *The fountainhead of friendship is love; for love can exist without friendship, but friendship without love, never. Love can be inspired by instinct, by a sense of obligation, by reason alone, by feeling alone, and sometimes by the two combined.* (On Spiritual Friendship 3, trans. Matarasso, 1993: 178; cf. SF 3.2: 88)

A spiritual friendship starts, Aelred informs his attentive students, 'when he, whom reason urges, should be loved because of the excellence of his virtue, steals into the soul of another by the mildness of his character and the charm of a praiseworthy life' (3.3, cited by Carmichael, 2004: 91; cf. SF 3.3: 89). The foundation of such a friendship, Aelred firmly tells them is, of course, the love of God to which everything else must be 'referred': spiritual love must keep trimming itself to suit the shape of the foundation which is God and there must be no hesitation 'to correct all the details on its model' (SF 3.5: 89). Building on the foundation must be subject to the closest scrutiny at all times.

Having clearly set out the underpinning of the building, which is friendship, Aelred addresses the practicalities. In the case of a specific friend, or particular friendships, he advises, considerable care must be taken in selection. The way in which friends are chosen is important for one's own happiness. Not all those whom we love can be invited into our friendship. Aelred sets out the reason for this circumspection in a soul-mate scenario:

> *Friendship is a twinning of minds and spirits where*
> *two become as one. Your friend is a second self from*
> *whom you withhold nothing, hide nothing, fear nothing.*
> (3, trans. Matarasso, 1993: 179; cf. SF 3.6: 89)

THE TRIANGULAR NATURE OF LOVE

When it comes to the nuts and bolts of friendship formation, there are four stages through which to pass viz. choice, testing, admission, agreement. The first three steps remind us of the *speculum* of charity, that higher level of love as a mirror:

> *The first essential, therefore, is to choose someone whom you judge suitable, then to try him, and finally to admit him to your friendship. For friendship should be stable, unfaltering in affection, holding a mirror to eternity.*
> (3, trans. Matarasso, 1993: 179; cf. SF 3.6: 89)

In the words of Aelred on acceptance and tolerance, we find those personal traits pinpointed in his relationship with the difficult monk: openheartedness, loving spiritual care, and persistence:

> *Once a friend has been accepted, however, that friend is to be so tolerated, so treated, and so encouraged that as long as he does not depart irrevocably from the foundation you have built, he should be so much yours and you so much his in bodily as well as in spiritual matters that there should be no separation of spirits, affection, will, or opinion.* (SF 3.7: 90)

The fourth stage is a reminder of the model of love discussed above in the section on Bernard and trinitarian love. There is to be concord, harmony, and charity in the agreement, and in such a consistent way is friendship perfected:

> *You notice then the four steps that lead to the perfection of friendship. The first is choice, the second testing, the third acceptance, and the fourth the highest agreement in things divine and human with a certain charity and good will.* (SF 3.8: 90)

Having grasped the four steps to friendship, the inevitable issue arises about what to do about the less likeable ones: the irascible, the fickle, the suspicious, and the verbose (SF 3.14: 91). Thus ensues a discussion between the three monks which shines a spotlight upon Aelred when challenged by Walter:

> *If I am not mistaken, I myself have seen you cultivate a friendship with an utterly irascible man, and with total dedication. Although he often hurt you, I have heard that to the last day of his life you never hurt him.* (SF 3.16: 91)

Aelred has no qualms about accepting such people as friends if he is assured of their affection. Mistakes are made and thoughtless remarks or actions can be excused in a friend (SF 3.17: 91). Aelred is also prepared, for the sake of maintaining friendship, to prefer the will of the friend to his own and to tolerate his transgression (SF3 20: 92). Momentary losses of friendship are not serious, as in the case of a burst of anger or a bitter word. Friendship ought not to be dissolved for such trifles. However, if a friend slanders, or betrays a secret or a confidence, or belittles you and poisons a friendship, then these are grounds for dissolution (SF 3.22–28: 92–95). But it should be a slow process, not an abrupt breaking, and respect and charity ought to be maintained, unless this person proves a menace to family, friends, and country, in which case immediate severing of the bond of familiarity is called for (SF 3.57–58).

In Aelred's worldview, mutual agreement transcends the usual problematics of friendship. Using the proverb, 'a friend loves always' (Prov. 17: 17), he makes the point earlier in the treatise that 'friendship is eternal if it is true, but if it ceases to exist, then, although it seemed to exist, it was not true friendship' (SF 1.21: 59). What he seems to mean by this is that true friendship will circumvent and overcome troubles and that if troubles do railroad friendship and it comes to an end then it was not a genuine friendship. Aelred's persuasive argument for the permanence of friendship has something to say to the fickle world of Facebook and Instagram, the community which would, at its hard core, be hard pressed to agree with the medieval monk that 'Though challenged, though injured, though tossed into the flames, though nailed to a cross, *a friend loves always*. And as our

THE TRIANGULAR NATURE OF LOVE

Jerome says, "*A friendship that can end was never true*"' (SF 1.21: 59). Here Aelred cites the Latin Church Father, theologian and monastic leader, Jerome (c. 347).

The application of the ideal of spiritual friendship is admirably translated to everyday life by a monk who has been through the mill himself in selecting and testing friends. Aelred sensitively shares his own experiences as a life model for his pupils and as a way of bringing his discourse to a conclusion. He recalls two friends: one stays the course while the other, chosen as 'a comrade and companion for the spiritual delights and attractions at the cloister' is 'snatched from me in the very beginning of our friendship.' As a youth he had 'bound' himself to this man, chosen for their 'likeness of character and similarity of interests.' Whatever the reason for the sudden disappearance of his brother monk, all is not lost as there remains the second, more worthy 'chosen friend' almost from boyhood to middle age. Aelred ruminates, 'in the light of memory', that this one, unlike the first, is more reliant upon reason, although affection is not absent, and ascends with him through all the steps of friendship (SF 3.119–120: 121). As abbot, Aelred raises him 'from a subordinate to a companion, from a companion to a friend, and from a friend to my dearest friend' (SF 3.121: 122). Aelred shares, as a teacher forming a student, the personal aspects of his journey to friendship with this man: '[I]f in this our friendship, which I have introduced by way of example, you discover something to imitate, make it serve your own purpose' (SF 3.127: 124)

Having outlined the various checks and balances, the weighing and considering in fashioning friendship, Aelred brings the dialogue to a close by reiterating the main point, which we found in the *Mirror of Charity*, that the love of self and the love of another are intricately woven together with the love for God as a threefold cord (MC 3.3.3–5: 223–224):

> Finally, to close our conference, with the sun setting fast, have no doubt that friendship grows out of love. If you do not love yourself, how can you love another? For from the likeness of

> the love with which you are personally dear to yourself, you ought to direct your love for your neighbour. But the one who exacts of himself or inflicts on himself anything disgraceful or dishonest does not love himself. (SF 3.128: 124)

AELRED OF RIEVAULX ON CHRIST AS THE THIRD BETWEEN FRIENDS

Having started, as it were, at the tail end of this treatise of three books, we must now approach the head and begin at the beginning. From the internal evidence of historical data, *On Spiritual Friendship* can be dated from some time after 1147 (during Bernard's lifetime) and completed in 1167. Its Prologue sets out Aelred's sources, narrative material, and method. As an adolescent boy confused and delighted at love and being loved, he had come across the classical text on friendship, Cicero's (106–43 BC) *De amicitia* (*On Friendship*) which had appealed by its beauty and soundness:

> Among the usual faults that often endanger youth, my mind surrendered wholly to affection [affectus] and became devoted to love. Nothing seemed sweeter to me, nothing more pleasant, nothing more valuable than to be loved and to love... [De amicitia]... a model to which I could recall my quest for many loves and affections. (SF Prol.1–3: 53; cf. MC 1.25.71: 128)

The narrative structure of the tractate is in three parts corresponding to the three books: the nature and origin of friendship; the greatness and limits of friendship; and, the development of friendship. The method of the tractate is based on Cicero i.e. the argument developed along the lines of a dialogue between teacher and student, in this case, the abbot as tutor and the monks as pupils.

CHRIST THE BEGINNING AND END OF FRIENDSHIP

As a novice in holy orders, Aelred begins to chew upon his slowly growing realisation that Cicero's thoughts on friendship do not taste the same to him as in previous years. He recognises that philosophical ideas which are 'not honeyed with the honey of the sweet name of Jesus' and 'not seasoned with the salt of the sacred Scriptures' do not win his affections. He wonders whether the authority of Scripture can support these pagan concepts (SF Prol.4–5: 54). He has no success with the writings of the early Church Fathers as they wished to love spiritually but were not able. Aelred resolves to rectify the situation and to write down his own 'rules for a pure and holy love' (SF Prol.6: 54). McEvoy asserts that this is 'the systematic treatise on Christian friendship which the Fathers… had failed to provide' (1981, cited in Carmichael, 2004: 80).

On Spiritual Friendship 1

The series of conversations among friends is set in a monastery at Wardon in Bedfordshire, a daughter house of Rievaulx (Carmichael, 2004: 81). The dramatis personae: Ivo, earnest, inquiring monk; Aelred, older and wiser abbot. This is an intimate conversation, and yet, there is another present:

> *You and I are here, and I hope that Christ is between us as a third. Now no one else is present to disturb the peace or to interrupt our friendly conversation. No voice, no noise invades our pleasant retreat. Yes, most beloved, open your heart now and pour whatever you please into the ears of a friend. Gratefully let us welcome the place, the time, and the leisure.'* (SF 1.1: 55)

Contrary to the pagan philosophers, Ivo wants to position spiritual friendship on the non-negotiable factor of Christ as its foundation as

> *the right kind of friendship between us, which should begin in Christ, be maintained according to Christ, and have its end and value referred to Christ. It is obvious indeed that Cicero was ignorant of the virtue of true friendship, since he was completely ignorant of Christ, who is the beginning and end of friendship.* (1.8: 57)

IN SEARCH OF FRIENDSHIP

Aelred applauds his pupil who has come up with the right answer and the most sublime statement of friendship:

> [I]t has been proved that friendship must begin in Christ, continue with Christ, and be perfected by Christ. (1.10: 57)

Aelred digs into the New Testament to support the argument that the early Christians were ready to go to the death for one another. (Acts 4:32). Being of one heart and soul they achieved 'the highest agreement in things divine and human, with charity and good will' (1.28–29, cf. Cicero, De amicitia 6.20: 60–61). These martyrs laid down their lives for their friends, the highest Christian ideal preached by Jesus Christ (1.30; John 15:13).

Carnal friendship (1.39–41) brings 'images of beautiful bodies or of voluptuous objects' (39: 63) and worldly friendship (1.42–44) 'fluctuates with fortune and chases coin' (42: 63). Spiritual friendship comes from the command of Jesus Christ to bear fruit and to love one another (1.46: 64; John 15:16–17).

> Now the spiritual, which we call true friendship, is desired not with an eye to any worldly profit or for any extraneous reason, but for its own natural worth and for the emotion of the human heart, so that its fruit and its reward is nothing but itself. (1.45: 64)

The origin of friendship is within the nature of God. God being the cause of every living thing so designed his creation that all are linked and joined in unity to share the unity which is in God himself. Here are the imprints of the earlier trinitarian theology discussed above:

> Thus from him who is supremely and uniquely one, all should be allotted some trace of his unity. For this reason, he left no class of creatures isolated, but from the many he linked each one in a kind of society. (1.53: 65)

The important principle Aelred is insisting upon is this: from angels to animals to human beings there are communal societies of groups and classes in loving attachments of actions and sounds, which resemble friendship (1.55: 66). These societies reflect the society of God himself, the Three in One. Friendship is part of the order of creation, but it exists as an image of God only among angels and human creatures (Dutton, 2010: 42). As far as human friendship goes, the precept of equality is clearly stated both in gender and in general terms. The first pair were friends as an image of God without hierarchy or boundaries:

> *In a beautiful way, then, from the side of the first human a second was produced [Gen. 2:21–22], so that nature might teach that all are equal or, as it were, collateral, and that among human beings—and this is a property of friendship— there exists neither superior nor inferior.* (1.57: 66)

This statement may be seen as an unintentional elaboration on Bernard's message to his brothers that Jesus himself emphasised equality by calling his disciples his friends (John 15:15):

> Do you see that even majesty yields to love? That is how it is, brothers. Love neither looks up to nor looks down on anybody. It regards as equal all who love each other truly, bringing together in itself the lofty and the lowly. (SS 59 1.2, trans. Walsh, 1979, 3: 121)

If friendship is, as it were, hardwired into the human community, then it follows that such bonds may be used for good or ill, a point Aelred teases out thoroughly in Book 2, backing up the pitfalls and joys of relationship by means of biblical precedents and examples. Ungodly soul ties, disguised as friendship are actually 'loathsome social contracts' leading to evil acts (1.60: 67).

Aelred begins to wind up the dialogue with his monk in a most intriguing process of deduction. If the divine nature of friendship is like the other excellent virtues and second only to wisdom (drawing on the Ciceronian precept that nothing is better than friendship

IN SEARCH OF FRIENDSHIP

except wisdom), in fact so close or filled with wisdom, then one can almost say that friendship is 'nothing other than wisdom' (1.64–66: 68, cf. Cicero De amicitia.20, in Carmichael, 2004: 84–85). Here, however, the virtue of wisdom is being transposed from a pagan, human attribute and elevated into a divine attribute i.e. *Sophia* examined earlier in the chapter. *Sophia* or Wisdom is an attribute of God, in fact another name for God. This sudden shift is problematic for Ivo. He knows that 'God is love', *Deus caritas est* (1 John 4:16) and that *caritas*, charity is the supreme virtue. By charity we welcome all, even enemies; by friendship only those to whom we entrust ourselves (cf.1.31–32: 61). Is Aelred asking him to accept a statement he has hitherto never contemplated?

> *To what does this lead? Should I say of friendship what*
> *John, the friend of Jesus, said of charity, 'God is friendship'?*
> *[Deus amicitia est]* (1.69: 69, cf. 1 John 4:16)

Aelred concedes that truly this statement is indeed a novel idea and has no scriptural authority i.e. we cannot say 'God is friendship' as we would say 'God is love'. Aelred does, however, want to attribute the rest of the verse to friendship:

> *The rest of that verse about charity, however, I surely do not*
> *hesitate to attribute to friendship because the one who remains in*
> *friendship remains in God, and God in him.* (1.70: 69; 1 John 4:16)

Aelred has previously rebutted this misleading concept of friendship being charity when Ivo tested him earlier:

> *Are we to conclude, then, that there is no distinction*
> *between friendship and charity?* (1.31: 61)

Aelred protests the simple deduction by exclaiming:

> *On the contrary, the greatest distinction! Divine authority*

> *commands that many more be received to the clasp of charity than to the embrace of friendship. By the law of charity we are ordered to welcome into the bosom of love not only our friends but also our enemies. But we call friends only those to whom we have no qualms about entrusting our heart and all its contents. (1.32: 61)*

Here is the great commandment of Jesus Christ to love one's enemies and to pray for persecutors (Matt. 5:44), to give away cloaks and money with gifts of compassion for thieves, borrowers, and malingers (Luke 6:27–35). But none of this is friendship, which is reserved for the intimates one chooses.

Carmichael gives a helpful summarary of the debate in modern scholarship around the notion that 'God is friendship', as this is the idea usually associated with the treatise (2004: 85–87). Outside the orbit of scholarship we note that this idea is one which the LGBT community wholeheartedly embraces. Accepting that God loves all as friends should guard us from particularism and we should love all equally (not a view Aelred espouses, as we have seen). Accepting that God is friendship must lead to exploring the Persons in the Trinity as friends (not a question which Aelred investigates apart from the Holy Spirit as the love between Father and Son). Accepting that God is friendship is a passage to Christ as both the mediator of true friendship and its location (not an opinion Aelred specifically addresses). Dutton acknowledges that although Aelred was probably keen to make a connection between God and friendship in the way described, he is prevented from making this speculative leap on the grounds of the authority of Scripture. God cannot be drawn into such an equivalence as to do so would limit God who is always entirely other:

> *The answer to Ivo's repeated inquiry, then, is a simple no, a recognition that while God created friendship as part of human experience and allows himself to be met and loved forever through friendship, he remains always other. (2010: 44–45)*

IN SEARCH OF FRIENDSHIP

From the triangular nature of friendship we have ascertained first, the importance of a correct and life-giving theology of the Trinity, and especially the Holy Spirit as the bond of love between humans and God. Secondly, we have realised that for human friendship to be permanent and of eternal value, the presence of Jesus is of primary significance. We have seen that spiritual friendship has a divine origin and, therefore, a purpose beyond that of naturally selected friends, dynamic as these can be and not to be disdained. Such divinely appointed friendships can move mountains, walk on water and be catalysts for change. Called by God to be companions with him for good, friendships of this order must keep, as their closest friend, the Lord himself: Christ between friends. Without that spark the world enters in and the friendship is tainted with ungodly desires. Holiness is all. Therefore, a first principle must be established from Bernardine piety: God is the peerless and matchless friend. From this point of view we proceed to Chapter 3 and to the explosive quality of friendship in public life.

Chapter 3

FRIENDSHIP IN THE PUBLIC SQUARE

'I'm so small,' said the mole.
'Yes,' said the boy, 'but you make a huge difference.'

Having established as a first principle God as the matchless and peerless friend who allows human beings to cultivate friendships of charity, we must now engage with the question of the divine purpose in matching friends. To this end we need to grapple with the monumental edifice which is the life and work of the Cistercian monk, in order to comprehend the sheer weightiness of Bernard's relationships in affairs both spiritual and temporal. We begin this review on the Bernardine foundation and starting point that God desires intimacy above all other intimates, that we are to be God's friends first and foremost. This tenet is perfectly captured in Sermon 59 on the Song of Songs, Bernard's commentary on the voice of the turtle-dove's cooing in our land (Songs 2:12):

> Notice then the utter happiness of hearing the God of heaven say: 'in our land'… He has done much for the earth, much for the bride, whom he has been pleased to take to himself from the earth. 'In our

> land', he says. This is clearly not the language of domination but of fellowship and intimate friendship. (1.1 trans. Walsh, 1979: 4, 120)

In contemplating love for God and others in Bernard of Clairvaux, we cannot escape the immense impact of his idealism. Holiness of life is his standard, moral purity his vision and, in the overlap of sacred and secular spheres of influence, he stands tall above his contemporaries—a measure against which the laxity of churchmen of the previous generations falls far short. The world of the saintly Abbot is limitless, encompassing the closed quarters of the abbey, infiltrating by stealth the conspiratorial corridors of ecclesiastical power, breaching the defences of kings and emperors, and still sounding today a clarion call to sanctity. What is the secret of his authority, his ascendency to a position in Europe as a much sought-after Christian talent?

We shall examine Bernard in the public square under three headings: Bernard as censor in the twelfth century; Bernard as friend in monastic reform; Bernard as God's friend in society. However, before engaging with these important subjects, we must look to Bernard the monk, to his interior life and to the impulses which gave impetus to what he did.

Bernard's concentration was, in the first instance, not on the outside world, but on the motives buried in his own heart. Closeness to God caused a closing off from society. The clothing he wore, the woollen white tunic, the tonsured head and the sparse diet set him apart. It is from this state of self-abasement that the monastic obligation of charity—to love the world—is fulfilled. Yet, it cannot be fulfilled by leaving the monastery. The Rule of Benedict is quite clear: a brother sent on some errand is expected to return to the monastery that same day (RB 51: 76). A brother may be sent on an errand by the abbot, but any brother who deigns to leave the enclosure without permission, on some trivial matter, has broken the Rule (RB 67: 98). And yet, Bernard is often away from his cell, bent on calls from those outside the confines of Clairvaux. How does he square his engagements in the public square with the responsibilities to the community he leaves behind? How does he marry his commitment to Christ and his contemplative prayer with a zeal for church order and matters of state?

From the point of view of a non-religious (i.e. not a monastic) lay person, the matter is quite straightforward. Jean-François Leroux-Dhuys, a French journalist, museum creator and architectural critic puts it thus:

> For Bernard of Clairvaux, filled with the principles at the basis of Christianity, political action and religious action were one. If the place of the Church in the world depended on it, he was quite prepared to become involved, even to the detriment of the monastic vows that obliged him to keep within the walls of his cloister. (Trans. Clegg et.al., 1998: 34)

At first glance, the felicitous ease in which political and religious agency are combined in this analysis is commendable; however, this synthesis does little to show the tremendous, strenuous, and costly passage which brough Bernard to this place in history. Before proceeding to the question of influential friendship and contact outside the monastery walls, it is important that we understand the root of the convictions which were the impulse for his actions. For this, we must turn to his own writings and especially to the treatise *De gratia et libero arbitrio* (*On Grace and Free Choice*), which provides the justification for his conduct.

On Grace and Free Choice
The dissertation treats of the essential problem of grace and freedom in the Letter to the Romans. As an early work written in about the year 1128, it must be seen in the light of the choices Bernard was making on the cusp of his entry into public spheres of influence. Urged by his great friend, William of Saint Thierry, to whom he addresses the script, Bernard sets out his dogma to the monastic theologian, himself an expert on grace and free will.

In a roundabout way, the treatise presents an argument whereby the acceptance of God's gift of grace to choose is in itself a choice. Having chosen grace, and then by means of that grace the freedom to choose, Bernard opens the way to interpret his call. The logic appears irrefutable: the more intense his work in the public square, the more the reliance upon God's grace in free choice. The genesis of the treatise is interesting. As with many of Bernard's works—made more intriguing by the circles of acquaintances and friendships stimulating his thinking and writing more than scholarly doctrinal disputes—this piece appears to have been inspired by a casual conversation. It is thus entirely relevant to the day.

Bernard was once conversing with others on his experience of the grace of God which simply propelled him along in the good way towards perfection. A bystander listening in asks the question, pertinent to the medieval mind but one which has troubled theologians through the centuries, namely, the role of human freedom:

> 'What part do you play, then… or what reward or
> prize do you hope for, if it is all God's work?'

Bernard parries: 'What do you think yourself?' To which comes the reply: 'Glorify God… who freely went before you, aroused and set you moving; and then live a worthy life to prove your gratitude for kindnesses received and your suitability for receiving more' (GFC 1.1: 53).

Bernard is pleased with this 'sound advice' but wishes to know *how* all this good living is to be accomplished. He argues that he needs the assistance of the Spirit as well as belief in his own good will. The bystander requires clarity on this point regarding the will, articulating the commonly held belief that merits, or good works, add spiritual 'brownie points' to the hope of salvation.

Bernard is astounded:

> 'What? Did you imagine that you can create your own merits,
> that you can be saved by your own righteousness?' (1.1: 54)

Clearly, the answer is a resounding 'No' and the question rhetorical as Bernard anticipates his interlocutor, setting out his view on the cooperation of free choice and grace:

> *'Maybe you are saying: "What part, then, does free choice play?" I shall answer you in one word: it is saved. Take away free choice and there is nothing to be saved. Take away grace and there is no means of saving. Without the two combined, this work cannot be done.'* (1.2: 54)

Bernard expounds on his theme: God's grace is the operating principle; free choice is the object of grace, which is free to receive, or not. The recipient will always be free to choose, to give consent to the operation of grace. Therefore, as free choice voluntarily cooperates with grace it is saved. Voluntary consent is not forced or coerced: if the will is compelled there is violent, not voluntary, consent. If the will consents, there is freedom. This is what Bernard understands by the term 'free choice' (1.2: 54–56).

Towards the end of the treatise Bernard feels that he ought to reiterate that the fault is in us, in we who are prone to evil and to sin, and that mercy alone saves. The good we do is through grace and not of ourselves. Merits come from God as gifts in the present life and we await their reward as a promise in eternal life (13.42-43:100–101).

Having established that, for Bernard, the human decision to cooperate with God entails choosing the way ahead by grace freely given, we are in a position to dwell upon the seriousness of his choices. We must, however, be mindful of the times in which he lived as a precursor to grasping the public square and his influence in it. His passage through it, remarkable as this is, was eased by the structure of society and the arrangement of its feudal systems. These observations are a backdrop to an analysis of public friendship.

BERNARD AS CENSOR IN THE TWELFTH CENTURY

The agrarian civil society of the twelfth century is aeons away from our fast-paced technological global village—our twenty-first century home. A medieval map, the Ebstorf Map of the World, depicts Asia, Europe, and Africa in a circle with Jerusalem as the central point, the surface of the earth a myriad of biblical, mythical, and historical events. Everything is oriented to the east, to Christ's earthly origins, from whence spiritual illumination will come. The earth floats in water and is surrounded by the starry firmament of the vast heavens: the infinite, the fixed and immovable reality of the Middle Ages (Schipperges, 1998: 10–12). But the world, too, is vast and open to horizons of physical, mental, and spiritual possibilities. Europe is on the move: epoch-making processes, shifts in power, stronger towns and long-distance commerce, the movement of scholars from one school to another, and troubadours spreading their tradition throughout Europe.

Heinrich Schipperges, a leading expert in the medieval period declares: 'Even the mystics of the Twelfth Century were not ineffectual solitaries, for their insights and writings found a growing audience and inspired many followers' (1998: 11). Monasteries were not cut off from the world but part of a network of feudal ties and obligations, and integral to the development of the 'mechanical arts' of hunting, fishing, gardening, architecture, the mill, the workshop and practical medicine. Abbesses and abbots were powerful figures, employers of labour, generating large incomes from their estates. And when it came to innovation and new thinking around the feudal tradition, it was the Cistercians who threw open their doors to hundreds of illiterate lay brothers, whose status it would be to remain in a state of illiteracy, forever peasants segregated from their brother monks, accepted into the order by virtue of the sweat of their brow in overseeing the granges, workshops and domestic chores in the abbey (Leroux-Dhuys, trans. Clegg et.al., 1998: 73).

The monastic ideal, the highest expression of human striving and still the 'vital force' in the twelfth century, was obedience and contemplation on the life of the spirit (Keen, 1968: 97). Herein was the driving impetus for the mushrooming reform movements and a reason for the first of the two triumphs of the twelfth century viz. the growth of the religious orders, the second being the universities. Bernard stood, preached, and wrote at the interface of these two fresh advances.

For Bernard, trained in the cloister, the love of learning and the desire for God were two sides of the same coin. Key to this understanding was the notion of revelation through the Spirit of God which promoted love for God, and response to that love came about through meditation upon Scripture and study of the Church Fathers. These hallowed texts became the focus of the schoolmen of the universities, the cathedral schools, and the logicians, who applied methods of reason to the sacred truths, questioning, speculating, digging deeper. The rise of the university (1150) and the procedures of scholarly debate functioned as a system of reasoning known as dialectic and structured as question + argument + conclusion. The new urban schools and the social realities of the culture brought about 'a doctrinal and moral elaboration to the substance of the word of God', the assumption that divine mystery can be understood by intellectual procedures (Gilson, 1968: xvi–xvii).

A more or less universally held view is that Bernard of Clairvaux is the last of the Church Fathers because he wrote without dialectic (Knowles, 1962: 141). Maurice Keen, erstwhile Fellow of medieval history at Balliol, analyses 'his own intense religious conviction' which inspired the famous confrontation with Peter Abelard (1079–1142), the monk, philosopher and theologian of the School of Paris, secured his condemnation for heresy by the pope and 'broke him, as a man, for ever. He acted because he thought he saw in Abelard's logic danger to the faith' (1968: 97).

Bernard's ability to seize the initiative in an age of unstable kingdoms and reshaping of local powers brought his leadership centre stage (Leroux-Dhuys, trans. Clegg et.al., 1998: 33). The British historian, Margaret Deanesly lists several of his important interventions: reproved the laxity of the French royal Abbey of St

Denis; rebuked the French king for expelling the bishop of Paris; drew various prelates to a more spiritual life; fearless in reprehending kings or nobles on moral issues or for cruelty to peasants; called on to confute heretics and to arbitrate in spiritual and secular disputes; an immense correspondence with men and women all over Europe; wrote the treatise *De consideratione*, parts of which dealt with the corrupt system of indulgence and papal provision to benefices (1954: 124). Deanesly concludes that, as a monastic reformer in what has become known as the Twelfth Century Renaissance, Bernard of Clairvaux 'not merely inspired his own order, but through mere belief in his courage, disinterestedness and devotion, he became a sort of censor to western Christendom, more respected than either pope or emperor.' (128). We see his censorship, or lack of it in the following texts as Bernard speaks to power.

COUNSELLOR AND CENSOR TO LEADERS

A good example of Bernard's courage as a leader is shown in his counsel of Pope Eugenius III (d.1153), whose speedy election as Pope in 1145 put a Cistercian in power. Bernard, from his rural retreat, cogitating in silence these unexpected developments, seizes the moment to make his request of the newly elevated pontiff, a matter which will be examined in the chapter under a different head. At present the heart of the question is the role reversal lightly and respectfully alluded to by the abbot. The importance of this cannot be more clearly stated as it shows the shift in power, the change in relationship and yet the tenacity of Bernard to hold his friend accountable. He feels he has the right as, only ten years before, Eugenius (then Bernardo) had followed Bernard to Clairvaux, becoming a lowly Cistercian under his leadership, before being appointed Abbot of Tre Fontan. The letter has inklings of anxious concern for his former monk's aptitude, a father who cannot quite believe that his son has achieved such greatness.

Letter 205

The salutation reads: 'To his most loving father and lord, Eugenius'

(1: 277). The 'securing of good will' portion of the letter emphasises the restraint in which Bernard has waited for news of the papal election. Now he is free to rejoice without envy, at the same time pointing out that he is the progenitor of the Pope's salvation:

> I dare not dare to call you a son any longer. You were my son, but now you have become my father. I was your father, but now I have become your son. You who came after me have been preferred before me. But I am not jealous, for I am sure that you who not only came after me but also, in a manner, through me, will make up in your person for what is lacking to me. For, if you will pardon my saying so, it was I who, as it were, begot you in the Gospel. What is it that I hope will be my joy and a glorious crown for me? It is you before God. A wise son is the pride of his father. (Le 1: 277)

The spiritual connection between these two men is profound. Despite the change in ecclesial rank, Bernard cannot quite let go of a father's concern for his son. In the 'narration' portion of the letter we have insight into his angst and feel his admonition expressed graphically but with great tenderness:

> Although I have laid aside the name of father, neither the fears nor the anxieties of a father have left me, least of all the affection and heart of a father. When I think of the heights to which you have been lifted up, I fear a fall. When I think of your great dignity, I look down into the jaws of the gulf that yawns before you. When I ponder on the honour which is yours, I fear the danger which is at hand... So you have gone up on high. But do not let that make you high-minded... You have been called to hold a high position, but not a safe one; a sublime position, but not a secure one. How terrible, how very terrible is the place you hold! The place where you stand is holy ground. (3: 278)

Here is Bernard at his kindliest and most concerned for his friend at the outset of his new role and rank in the Church. It transpires that his worry about Eugenius is not without substance. He has cause for concern and begins almost immediately a treatise directed to the pope, a work of five books completed within the next decade. The treatise, *Five Books on Consideration: Advice to a Pope* (*De consideratione*) advises Eugenius to pursue his spiritual life amid the daily pressure of papal affairs.

On Consideration

To be noted as background to the work (cf. Kennan 1976: 16–17) is the sheer brilliance with which the treatise tackles the paradox at the centre of Eugenius' roles, one which Bernard recognises and addresses, not by means of a choice between two alternatives, but as a middle path. The paradox of Eugenius the Cistercian monk, dedicated to the interior life of contemplative prayer, and Eugenius the pope responsible for the morality of the strong, the safety of the Holy Land, the protection of the monasteries, and the administration of the entire papacy. Bernard's turn to the median way as a solution develops the classical rule of virtue, which is moderation in everything—the yardstick for him of reform.

Our purpose is the friendship between the two leaders, which the texts examined from Book 1 attempt to draw out. Bernard wishes to understand the term 'consideration', which had been used by Gregory the Great in his *Regula Pastoralis* to describe the task of a bishop. The treatise is a response to that question (Evans, 1987: 145). The essence of consideration is the verse from the psalm, 'Be still and know that I am God' (Psa. 45:11 sic). Consideration is not contemplation but it is the quest for truth.

Bernard's initial instruction to Eugenius, and indeed to anyone who holds high office, is to clear the diary of distractions. If this is not done the heart will deteriorate, neither fearing God nor respecting man, a 'state to which these cursed demands can bring you if you continue, as you have begun, to devote yourself totally to them, leaving no time or energy for yourself.' Metaphorically throwing up his hands, Bernard exclaims: 'What do all these things produce but spiders' webs?' (Csi 1.2.3, trans. Anderson, 1976: 28–29).

Day and night people press in with requests, there is no space to rest, and the poor body is driven (1.3.4: 29). And everywhere 'confusion and noise, the yoke of your servitude, bear down upon you' (1.3.4: 31).

In a devastating comparison with Paul, Bernard tackles the clamouring agitators, taking the Pope to task by asking rhetorically whether the Apostle had any truck with those seeking financial gain in exchange for church offices. This is a reference to the prevalent practice of simony, the buying and selling of church positions, a pressure point for Eugenius, who seems to be in bondage to this practice, or at least overwhelmed by the demands of such persons:

> *Do not reply now with the words of the Apostle: 'Although I was free from all men, I made myself a slave to all.' This is hardly your situation. Did Paul in his slavery aid men in the acquisition of mere financial gain? Were the ambitious, the avaricious, the simoniacal, the sacrilegious, the fornicating, the incestuous and every other kind of monstrous person crowding around him from every corner of the earth to obtain or retain ecclesiastical honours by his apostolic authority?... If you would listen instead to another of his statements: 'You were bought for a price, do not become slaves of men.'* (1.4.5: 31)

Bernard follows through his papal admonition by telling Eugenius that to 'sweat over such affairs for the likes of these' is servile and unworthy of the Supreme Pontiff (1.4.5: 31). He then reminds the pope of his true task, to teach the ways of the Gospel:

> *Tell me this, when are we to pray or to teach the people? When are we to build up the Church or meditate on the law?... Tell me, therefore, how can you, as bishop and shepherd of souls, allow the Law to stand silent before you while others rattle on? I am at a loss if this perversity does not cause you anxiety.* (1.4.5: 31–32).

Having given the Pope a light dressing down for neglecting his

IN SEARCH OF FRIENDSHIP

papal role as teacher of the ways of God, Bernard then turns to his Cistercian call, to the primary principle of loving God above all else. From this devotional intimacy will overflow the work for God. From consideration, from finding the truth in the 'bosom which receives everyone', will come a benefit which will positively affect the work for others. From being a friend of God to being a friend to others, in actions rightly considered before execution.

> Listen to what I condemn and to what I suggest. If you apply all your experiences and knowledge to activity and have nothing for consideration, do I praise you? I do not. … Certainly, an action suffers if not preceded by consideration. If you want to belong totally to all men in the likeness of him who was made all things to all men, I praise your devotion to mankind, but only if it is complete. Now, how can it be complete when you have excluded yourself? You too are a man. For your devotion to be whole and complete, let yourself be gathered into that bosom which receives everyone. (1.5.6: 33)

Bernard ends his warning to the beleaguered Pope with inspiring words: Eugenius is not to be so busy with activity which consumes his whole being that he cannot give himself to the art of consideration, of making sense of things, of finding truth. Bernard is asking the Pope for an inward, personal response to God, directing him to find the 'sweet spot' of his monastic call:

> It is one thing to rush headlong into these affairs when there is an urgent reason, but it is another, entirely, to dwell on them as if they were important and worthy of this kind of papal attention. I must express these thoughts and many like them if I am to speak forcefully, righteously and with sincerity. But since these are evil days, it is enough to have warned you not to give yourself completely or continually to activity and to lay aside something of yourself—your attention and your time—to consideration. (1:7.8)

In the fifth and final book Bernard turns his attention to that which is above viz. the eternal gaze, the other side of action, that of examination. In so doing he cuts a swathe through the field of Eugenius' soul: on the one hand, the monastic life and on the other, the duties of papal office. The middle path is found by Bernard because both states are dependent for their sustenance and life upon the invisible realm of God. All action—monastic or papal—all visible affairs of this life ought to be ordered and lived in the light of the invisible, in the illumination of eternity, and this, dear Eugenius, is to return to your homeland!

> *There is no way in which you can act upon those things which always exist in the same way and which will be the same for all eternity (some of these have even been the same from all eternity). And I would wish, most wise Eugene, that you be intelligent enough to realise that your consideration wanders whenever it turns from these things to lesser, visible things, whether they be regarded as a source of knowledge, or sought for practical application, or administered or employed officially. However, if your consideration deals with these things so that through them it seeks what is above, it does not go into exile: to consider in this way is to return to one's homeland.* (5.2.1 55–56)

So ends the papal lesson of *De consideratione*, a work which will be mentioned in the study of the spiritual disciplines in Chapter 4. Very briefly, we alight on an instance which, once again, shows the close allegiance between Bernard and Eugenius, almost a papal concession to the wisdom of his fellow Abbot. The matter revolves around a piece of writing, *Scivias* ('Know the Ways'), which is a reply to Abelard's work, *Sci te ipsum* ('Know yourself'). The topic is as controversial as the authors, in that both Abelard—discussed above as a rationalist philosopher condemned for heresy—and Hildegard, a woman abbess and prophet, are outstanding, radical influencers in twelfth-century Europe, but in different ways. Abelard is a scholastic of the urban university schools; Hildegard is a monastic enclosed in her order and schooled in its disciplines of learning. Having ousted Abelard shall the Church embrace Hildegard?

Hildegard of Bingen (1098–1179) the German prophet, Sybil of the Rhine, and Benedictine Abbess of Mont St Rupert, is as influential as Bernard in the sheer volume of writing and correspondence to heads of state, emperors, kings, popes, and prelates. She is a visionary among many visionaries of that time, but she is also *magister* i.e. teacher with political power but, as a woman, subject to male authority. Her potentially controversial prophetic writing is validated by Eugenius III, due in no small measure to the patronage of Bernard (Campbell, 2012: 7–9). Their correspondence is interesting. Clearly, Hildegard knows that to gain support from this powerful male personage is to her advantage and she writes to him, as one visionary to another in laudatory praise: 'You move about, but you sustain others. You are assuredly an eagle looking into the sun.' (EP 91.1.48–9, trans. Campbell, 2012:105).

Letter 390

Bernard's reply to the Abbess seems ideally suited to her purpose, recognising her charism or gift of prophecy:

> To his beloved daughter in Christ, Hildegarde… I congratulate you on the grace of God that is in you and admonish you to regard it as a gift and to respond to it with all humility and devotion… How could I presume to teach or advise you who are favoured with hidden knowledge… for you are said to be able to search the secrets of heaven and to discern by the light of the Holy Spirit things that are beyond the knowledge of man. (460)

These two mighty mystics appear to be on the same side of the debate, that revelation is given and received by means of the anointing of the Spirit of God (monastic theology) and not through dialectical speculative reasoning (the university and cathedral schools). Cautious critics credit Bernard with 'a certain circumspection', an ambivalence which did not overtly embrace or champion Hildegard's visions but did not attack them, thereby opening the door for papal approval (James, 1998: 460; McGuire, 2020: 268). A kind critic remarks on Bernard's restraint, which is not curt but straightforward and considers the wider spiritual society, reassuring suspicious churchmen of her visions by his defence of a woman (Leclercq, 1989: 63–66).

Perhaps at the heart of the issue is less a question of which version of Bernard's letter is consulted—the longer or the shorter—as to which view is preferred, but more the fact that he was a man on a mission, a reformer of monasticism. As a Benedictine woman, Hildegard would have bypassed his notice, as indeed he bypassed Bingen twice on his journeys without visiting her abbey. As Leclercq notes (1989: 62), he preferred the mandates from a pope to the oracles of a woman and knew the value of the hierarchy of church life—as we have seen in his instruction of Eugenius. An extraordinarily humble man of his times, neither a pope nor a prince, but a simple abbot without official standing in the hierarchies of power, yet standing out as a contemplative who mightily influenced the world of action but also led the Christian world, in the first half of the twelfth century, in so many aspects of the life of that time. (Sommerfeldt, 1991: xiii–xiv). It is the imprint of Bernard's character and vision upon the advance of the monastic programme that is intriguing.

BERNARD AS FRIEND IN MONASTIC REFORM

An historical overview or narration of Bernard's reform of monasticism is not within the scope of this chapter, which is concerned with an investigation of friendship as a force for innovative change. However, one or two introductory remarks will set the scene for such an examination as we stand with Bernard on the threshold of something new, something completely different when we think about the age of upheaval which is the twelfth century. The excitement of cross-pollination of ideas through new trade relations between towns and countries and the growth of the intellectual property of Europe through the universities are catalysts for change. There is an international flavour to the comings and goings: From mainland Europe to the Middle East and across the Channel to England. These routes and avenues give grist to the mill and accelerate monastic reform. Dyed in the wool old Europe is on the cusp of of the new and Bernard is part forerunner, part traditionalist—a hybrid of new and old.

Before the advent of Bernard the monk, but in the year of his birth (1090), there is established the New Monastery of Cîteaux in the marshy forest between Nuits-Saint-Georges and the Saône river. Despite their efforts at a more rigorous application of the Benedictine Rule, the new venture did not attract new vocations, in fact it declined. With the patronage of the Duke of Burgundy a parcel of land is given them and the small group moves to Saint-Nicolas-lès-Cîteaux (Côte-d'Or) in about 1101. In 1119 the Order of Cîteaux (Cistercian) is born by papal decree, whose constitution preserves the independence of each abbey established, departing from the feudal hierarchical system which was the norm for all other Benedictine orders. (Leroux-Dhuys, 1998: 25–28). The interest among the Burgundian nobility is peaked by the newcomers, whose radical way of life attracts the attention of one of their number, Bernard of Fontaines, who arrives with a cohort of family and friends in 1113 (see Chapter 1).

In 1115 Bernard is sent out and, on the border of Burgundy and Champagne, opens up the clearing of Val d' Absinthe (Wormwood), establishing the monastery of Clairvaux, a community of roughly two dozen members (Holdsworth, 2011: 169). There is an electrifying explosion of life and and expansion is at such a pace that in less than 40 years at the time of his death in 1153, Clairvaux comprised 800 monks and lay brothers; 69 monasteries and 100 of their daughter houses are dependent upon Clairvaux as their mother house (Leroux-Dhuys, 1998: 174). Holdsworth has a conservative estimate based on Geoffrey of Auxerre: 200 monks and 500 lay brothers; 63 daughter houses of which 23 affiliates spread out over most of western Europe, France, Italy, Spain, the Empire, Scandinavia, Britain, and Ireland

(2011: 169). We may well inquire as to the secret of this unusual diaspora.

It is Bernard's impulsive and persuasive dynamic which is the new spirituality influencing secular literature—as we have seen in Chapter 2—challenging and invigorating the smug, static, and old Benedictine Order. At the heart of his movement are two powerful spiritual energies i.e. *restitutio*, the restoration of the Church and *restoratio*, the salvation of the soul. Two interwoven coils forming a double helix, a genetic code deeply ingrained within the body of Christ, the Church—Bernard's beloved Bride of Christ. Both impulses permeate the works, indelibly marking the writings, ringing clear as a bell in his sermons as the Abbot instructs, implores, chastens, and inspires men and women to devote themselves to love of Christ and service in his vineyard. That which has grown stale in the life and worship of the Church must make way for fresh interpretations of liturgical practice. That which has passed for personal piety must give over to ascetical purity.

Gillian Evans, author of the Foreword and translator of a volume of Bernard's selected works is Emeritus Professor of Medieval Theology and Intellectual History at the University of Cambridge. She writes insightfully of the lifetime of Bernard of Clairvaux which intersected one of the most spirited periods of monastic experiment in the medieval West:

> *Adults of mature experience, men who had been soldiers and landowners and their wives, were giving up their worldly positions to enter the religious life. Monasteries that had for many generations taken in the children given them by wealthy families and trained them now had to adapt to the demands of adult vocation and try to make monks and nuns of grown men and women, many of them unlettered and unprepared for the realities of the life they were entering.* (1987: 1)

These newcomers bring their life experience with them, stimulating reform of the older, more traditional ways. Evans opines that of any single individual, Bernard's influence in shaping monastic life and spirituality is probably the greatest. By example and preaching to hundreds of Cistercians, he acted out simplicity of life, balanced observation of the Rule, and ardour for God (2). But Bernard as a single individual is not alone; he had friends in high places and in low places. His life-force is shared with friends and his vision spreads. He is in good company with the wisdom of the biblical Preacher:

> *Two are better than one, for their partnership yields this advantage: if one falls, the other can help his companion up again; but woe betide the solitary person who when down has no partner to help him up. And if two lie side by side they keep each other warm; but how can one keep warm by himself? If anyone is alone, an assailant may overpower him, but two can resist; and a cord of three strands is not quickly snapped.* (Eccl. 4: 9–12)

We shall consider friendship in monastic reform under two heads, the two concepts noted above as *restitutio* (restitution of the Church) and *restoratio* (restoration of the soul). The friendship between Bernard and William of Saint Thierry acts as a kind of combustion burner in which their reforming zeal is fired, in which case we have primarily to do with *restitutio* and the health of the wider monastic community.

BERNARD AND WILLIAM OF SAINT THIERRY

The much-discussed friendship between Bernard and William of Saint Thierry is an obvious launchpad for rumours of reform. Two young pioneering abbots bonded by a common spiritual purpose to see the kingdom of God advance in their age—the warmth between Bernard and William a symbol of the flame of monasticism alive in the hand of God. William did much, in his writings and in his encouragement of Bernard— at times quite provocative—to advance the cause of monastic reform. William's account of the early years of Cîteaux and Clairvaux, written before his death in 1148, became

Book 1 of the *Vita prima* and is an honest portrayal of Bernard by a true friend. Books 2 by Arnald, Abbot of Bonneval, and Books 3, 4 and 5 by Geoffrey of Auxerre, Bernard's secretary, paint a picture of an older, almost legendary figure, designed, one suspects, to point up sanctity and readiness for canonisation (the process whereby a holy person is made a saint by the Roman Catholic Church). William's sketch is refreshingly intimate and 'remarkably frank on the first years of Bernard's abbacy, which saw him walking a knife-edge between psychological maturity and breakdown. The portrait of the young man who descended from his spiritual Sinai incapable of communicating with his monks on a level they could understand, and then despaired of his own inadequacy (Matarasso, 1993: 19).

In its infancy the friendship incubates the vision which will over time mature and ripen into the conquering and ever-expanding Cistercian Order. In the *Vita prima* William traces an outline of Clairvaux, the capital of a novel new asceticism in the monastic world and its Abbot whom he will follow to the ends of the earth!

Vita prima 1.5.25–26
There is the food prepared with beech leaves, the bread of barley and millet; the long night prayer watches and the cold; and Bernard in the pre-dawn standing outside in fervent intercession for the salvation of souls:

> As he stood in prayer, being in that state of spiritual desire
> we have just described, he suddenly saw, through half-closed
> eyes, such a multitude of men of all sorts and conditions
> come thronging down from the surrounding hills into the
> valley bottom that the valley itself could not hold them.
> Today the meaning is plain for all to see. (VP 1.5.26: 27)

Retrospectively, William sees the fulfilment of the vision of multitudes in the sheer volume of new recruits drawn as a moth to a candle to Clairvaux—as he himself was.

IN SEARCH OF FRIENDSHIP

Vita prima 1.7.26
As a Benedictine abbot, the older William—by a few years—seeks out Bernard, a fellow abbot already of some renown in the early stages of his abbacy. The visit finds the Cistercian recuperating from a near-fatal illness, most likely to have been brought on by his harsh diet, sleeplessness, and a tender disposition. He is living slightly apart in the grounds of Clairvaux in a sort of hovel, under special ecclesial dispensation, orchestrated by concerned friends in high places and his fellow monks (McGuire, 2020: 36–37). William is drawn immediately to him in a life-changing encounter. There is no way that he ever wishes to leave the sweet presence of this man. He longs to remain with him in this simplicity and poverty, serving him forever. There is something about Bernard which ignites a fire for God himself:

> I found him, when I first went to visit him with another abbot, in that little bothy of his, of the type normally built for lepers at public crossroads. And there I found him enjoying the freedom from all domestic cares, both indoor and outdoor, won for him by the order just described, with time for God and himself, and exulting as it were in the delights of paradise. As I stood in that royal chamber considering the dwelling and its inmate, as God is my witness, the place fired me with as much reverence as if I had gone in to the altar of God. So deeply affected was I by the aura of sweetness surrounding the man, so intense was my desire to live with him in that poverty and simplicity that, had the choice been given me that day, I should have wished for nothing more than to stay with him there for ever and wait upon him. (VP 1.7.26: 30)

Vita prima 1.7.34
The sense of an eternal space, a timelessness in the very air William breathes as he lodges with Bernard, is caught in his reminiscences: truly this abbot is a pattern of the ancient Desert Father:

> Unworthy though I was, I spent a few days with him, and

> wherever I turned my eyes I was amazed to see as it were
> a new heaven and a new earth, and the well-worn path
> trodden by the monks of old, our fathers out of Egypt, bearing
> the footprints left by men of our own time. (30–31)

In Bernard, William sees the origins of monasticism, and he is thrilled by what he feels. Here are the roots of a centuries-old tradition in a secession from his own fossilised Benedictine way. He feels the irresistible spell of the Bernardine mysticism, that somehow the monk is the go-between of earth and heaven for their age. The Cistercian and the Benedictine are drawn together in a friendship which is beyond themselves and for a higher purpose viz. the progression and flowering of monastic renewal.

That revival will require a new church for services of worship for the countless disciples converted to the monastic way who will come streaming in. William's belief that this greater glory in a greater building will be given to Bernard is a prompt for a passage in the Vita prima which recounts Bernard at prayer and hearing [in an auditory vision] the voices of a great many people passing by. On following them he comes to a spot overgrown with bushes to find choirs of men singing. This is the location for the building of the new church of Clairvaux (McGuire, 2020: 37). This supernatural vision of the future is followed by William's lyrical word-picture of the 'golden age' of Clairvaux as he looks back at the very first settlement.

Vita prima 1.7.35

Men once rich in this world's goods came to serve Christ in poverty, living for their brothers in communal comradeship. The huddle of huts clustered in the valley—joined-up humble hermits at work or prayer in silence:

> [I]n that very hive of activity, where none might be idle but
> each was busy at his appointed task, a midnight hush would
> greet the noontide visitor, broken only by work noises or the
> chanting of the office, as might be. This much-talked-of silence,

inspired such awe in laymen coming to the monastery that they were afraid to pass any remark that was not essential to their business, let alone a frivolous or improper one. (VP 1.7.35: 31)

William embroiders his earlier image of the 'well-worn path trodden by the monks of old' (VP 1.7.34: 31) in the figure of their founding father Benedict, prototype and model, whose life is the mainstay and whose Rule the basis for all monastic orders. Their huts stand for the cave in which he lived and the valley becomes a desert (just like the Desert Fathers of old) for each of the many men who lived there.

Here is the longing in William, exemplified in the life of Bernard, of a greater connection with his beginnings as a monk. He wants a return to the tougher regime, the immense desert silence, the lonely solitude, and the presence of God 'under the rule of love ordered by reason' (VP 1.7.35: 31). It is this which fires his longing to escape his abbatial duties and flee to Clairvaux. He sees that the Cistercian monks have stripped back the limitations of the old monastic ways to seek the one thing necessary for the vocation: to linger and gaze upon the face of God. Clairvaux and its stringently ascetical abbot represent all this to the Abbot of Saint Thierry. It is as though, 700 years on, Bernard is the new Benedict—such is the magnetic pull upon William.

Vita prima 1.8.38

But there is more: Benedict's Rule is based on a concept which is picked up by William.

> *And so we intend to establish a school for the Lord's service. In doing so we hope to demand nothing that is harsh, nothing oppressive.* (RB Prologue: 9)

The word for 'school' is *schola* with connotations of instruction, discipline, and progress (RB n.4: 110). William writes of a 'school of spiritual studies' in the almost-mythical 'far-famed and most beloved valley' where Bernard was the 'moving spirit of the house' (1.7.35, 8.38: 31).

If only, bewails William, Bernard had taken a leaf out of his own book and given himself the self-care, the same concern he showed toward the poor and weak, instead of going hammer and tongs 'like a torrent dammed and then unleashed' (VP 8.38: 32). Despite William's fussiness, the Vita prima shows that after his period of seclusion and withdrawal imposed by the order in his 'bothy' at the crossroads, Bernard never returned to the earlier austerity which had taken him there in the first place (Matarasso, 1993: 32).

The friendship between the two men is under the hammer: it is not a cushy ride. In the matter of monastic reform their vision is similar, their methods dissimilar. Their friendship could be said to be an illustration of the biblical proverb:

As iron sharpens iron,
so one person sharpens the wits of another.
(Prov. 27:17)

An Apologia for Abbot William
Elder discusses Bernard and William as allies (2011: 119–122). It is not quite clear who is leading who as each appears to use the other in achieving their own ends. Like pieces on a chessboard, they manoeuvre or outmanoeuvre one another. For example, it is William's displeasure incurred at the reading of Peter Abelard's theological books that sends him into a frenzied defence of orthodoxy, pushing Bernard to confront Abelard and leading, as we have seen, to the public humiliation and exclusion of the schoolman. The zeal in Bernard is equally persuasive and questionable. For example, by preventing the desperate William from attaining his heart's desire and joining the Cistercians, is Bernard deliberately keeping him engaged with other like-minded, black-robed Benedictine reformer-abbots? By so doing Bernard advances his own reform ideas which oppose the laxity of the monastery of Cluny, a cause close to his heart. In fact, it is William who approaches his

friend with a request that he write a tract which satirises the lax monastic habits of the Cluniac Order. Almost tongue in cheek, Bernard writes his piece for his friend who shares his passion for reform, calling it *An Apologia for Abbot William*.

Why should it matter? Why is there so much energy expended on what seems a trite matter of white or black robes, too many psalms sung, too little work with the hands, too many donations received, too much wealth and power? Bernard and William stand on the shoulders of the forerunners who began the shining move of austerity at Cîteaux as a protest against the 200-year-old Cluniac Order. The spirit of Cluny took to an extreme the splendour of ceremony in their magnificent buildings, carried their emotional spirituality to the nth degree in overabundant psalmody, stepped around the labour of intellectual study and degrading manual work, and grew in power with prelates and princes. The Cluniac interpretation of the Benedictine Rule exalts the majesty and fullness of transcendent divinity, apparent in their extravagantly splendid architecture. The Cîteaux/Cistercian reform interprets the Rule by glorifying God through manual labour (including the innovation of lay brothers to work the land), study (the building of libraries), silence (not constant psalmody) and simplicity (in the architectural design and layout of the monastic enclosure and church).

Bernard and William have the same goal and their friendship furthers their cause for reviving the pure spirit of the Benedictine Rule. In a nutshell, all this is *restitutio*, the restitution to the Orders of the original vision and plan of Benedict. But when all is said and done and the weightier business of monastic disputes and doctrinal debates are set aside it is William's affectionate insights into his friend's ability to love others, which is striking. For here, too, are the seeds of reform: the drawing out of others true spirituality, true religion. And this, it may be said, is the work of *restoratio*—the restoring of the individual soul to Christ's embrace.

William's depiction of Bernard's interior life may be understood in light of his earlier perception of Clairvaux as men living 'under the rule of love ordered by reason' (VP 1.7.35: 31). For he sees in

Bernard the exemplification of the spiritual exercises which were the measure by which he lived and which he passed on to his monks:

> As often as he could get away from business, he would be either praying, reading or writing, or else busied with teaching and forming the brothers [emphasis mine], or again, steadfast in meditation. (VP 3.1.2: 39)

A single phrase in William's account of his abbot friend at the height of his authority illuminates the esteem and veneration in which Bernard is held by all, brothers, and crowds alike. After a particularly strenuous (and public) exorcism of an evil spirit from a woman in the abbey church, we are told that the whole city 'yearned after him with love' (VP 2.3.14: 37). This adulation taxes the Abbot as William is quick to point out, mentioning with a friend's superior wisdom the psychological workings of his soul in the following passage.

Vita prima 3.7.22

> I often heard him confess to feeling, in the midst of the honours and marks of favour heaped on him by commoners and princes, that he had become someone else, or better, that he was absent and the whole thing as illusory as a dream. But when the simpler brothers confided in him trustingly, as was their way, and he had leisure to enjoy it with the unassuming friendliness he always showed, then he rejoiced to find himself again and recover his true identity. (40)

William is a spectator of the public persona but he has glimpses too of the kindliness, the 'friendliness' in the everyday conversations. His narrative has done much to preserve Bernard's simplicity of heart and desire to sustain the purity of the Benedictine way—a cause to which William is equally devoted and which binds them more closely than friends in the normal sense of the word.

FRIENDSHIP IN MONASTIC SKIRMISHES

Far from being the tranquil place of the romantic imagination, the cloister was too often both noisy and troublesome—at least inwardly if not outwardly—and out of step with the will of God. Resolution, restoring friendships, and repentance; these are signs of *restoratio*, the second of the two concepts and touching on the movements of the individual soul as they impact on friendship in monastic reform.

On occasion, Bernard goes into the field of monastic reform with both guns blazing, as is the case with an attempted rescue of a family member from the clutches of Cluny. This is his nephew, Robert, promised as a child to that order, but as an older boy and off his own bat deciding to follow in the footsteps of his famous relative. But no sooner is he in than he is out: finding life at Clairvaux restrictive and tiresome he is 'kidnapped' by a Cluny man and carried away. Bearing in mind that no letter is private in monastic family life, but read out loud, Bernard's missive is even more lethal as 'the first shot fired in the great controversy between the congregation of Cluny and the Cistercian reform' (James, 1998: 1).

Letter 1

The 29-year-old Bernard writes to Robert in terms of endearment and with his heart on his sleeve. He wishes to remove the grounds for dispute by writing humbly:

> *I who have been wounded am forced to recall him who wounded me; who have been spurned, him who spurned me; who have been smitten, him who struck the blow. In short I must cast myself at the feet of him who should cast himself at mine.* (Le 1: 1)

Here is Bernard reaching out, longing for his own kith and kin to be with him in his reform movement. He is grieved at the loss of a family friend. He tells Robert that he will not bear grudges or open old wounds. He is contrite as he feels that he was too strict with the young lad, and he takes full responsibility for his faults as abbot. He has changed. The incident with his nephew has altered their relationship. Robert may now see him, not as a harsh taskmaster but as a companion, in short, a friend (2: 2).

In his inimitable style, Bernard has covered the 'seeking assurance of good will' part of his letter. Now he gets down to the 'narration': the visit to Clairvaux by the Grand Prior of Cluny sent to entice wayward monks back home:

> *Outwardly he came in sheep's clothing, but within he was a ravening wolf... This wolf in sheep's clothing fascinated, allured, and flattered. He preached a new Gospel. He commended feasting and condemned fasting. He called voluntary poverty wretched and poured scorn upon fasts, vigils, silence, and manual labour.* (4: 4)

Bernard's opening shot is followed by a volley of live ammunition in a storm of protest at the deliberate deceit he discovers:

> *By such sophistries the too credulous boy was talked round, led astray and led off by his deceiver. He was brought to Cluny and trimmed, shaved, and washed. He was taken out of his rough, threadbare, and soiled habit, and clothed with a neat and new one. Then with what honour, triumph, and respect was he received into the community!... He was befriended, flattered, and congratulated by the whole fraternity. Everyone made merry over him as though they were victors dividing the booty.* (5: 4)

The family land promised to Cluny at the entry of Robert as a novice monk has already been possessed, and Bernard accuses the Cluniacs of prizing the land above the child. He wishes to announce emphatically that Robert has made a foolish choice by leaving him, having already made vows to the Cistercian Order. Bernard muses that Robert has been saved at the cost of persecuting himself and his order. This is war and it is unpleasant. Like the stolen baby brought to Solomon's wisdom (1 Kings 3:16-28), Bernard feels as though he has been robbed of his child by brother monks who ought to be friends:

> *You too were taken from my side, cut from me. My heart cannot forget you, half of it went with you, and what remains cannot but suffer. But our friends who have tried to do this thing… for what advantage of yours have they done it, for what necessity?* (9: 7)

Deep down in Bernard's psyche, there appears to be a figment of family loyalty, despite his vows of renunciation of ties for the sake of Christ. This natural bias, for good or ill, is evident in his dealings with his natural brother Bartholomew, whom he had excommunicated and banished from the abbey in a fit of pique (cf. Casey, 2011: 71). We are made aware of this issue only because Guy, Abbot of Trois-Fontaines (the first abbey planted from Clairvaux), is in a monastic pickle, having made a wrongheaded judgement and Bernard is his counsellor friend.

Letter 73

From the beginning the tone of the letter is sympathetic. Bernard is pastoral advisor to all his fellow abbots in the daughter houses of Clairvaux and takes seriously the reform of monasticism as *restoratio* (restoration of the soul). This is Bernard as Father Abbot, yet the expression 'from Brother Bernard' in the salutation identifies him as a monk—the implication being that he is a brother like them among brothers (cf. Heb. 4:15). He writes in a 'spirit of knowledge and pity' (Le: 103). For assuredly he has been in the exact same spot of bother. He will offer insight and consolation to Guy's distress by drawing on his own experience of falling into an error of judgement and his being brought to a place of submission to the will of the community and according to the Rule.

Bernard reveals that once, when Bartholomew had upset him, he had turned him out of the monastery with 'angry voice and threatening looks', only to find out that his brother had taken himself off to the abbey granges. Bernard's attempts to recall him are rebuffed as the miscreant stands steadfastly on the letter of the law i.e. the *Rule of Benedict*. Strictly speaking, he had not been given a fair trial or public hearing (RB 23: 44) and, therefore, technically has not been excluded. Is this a matter of sibling rebellion or is Bernard at fault for giving in to his natural moods? He writes openly and frankly:

> As I could not trust my own judgement in the matter owing to my natural feelings about it, I submitted it to the consideration of the brethren. And they, when I was absent, ruled that the brother should not be subjected to the discipline of the Rule on being received back, as his expulsion has not been according to the Rule. (2: 102–103)

Here is Bernard at his best and able to instruct Guy in a similar predicament with a recalcitrant monk (if indeed is the case as the story is not known). Here is the application of the abbot's role to restore the soul and bring back the lost, as laid down in the Rule:

> The abbot should exercise great care and extreme sensitivity, making every effort not to lose any of the sheep entrusted to him [even those of his own family]. (RB 27: 48)

As a postscript to the analysis of friendship in monastic skirmishes, with especial emphasis on the healing work of *restoratio*, we allude briefly to Geoffrey of Auxerre, Bernard's secretary and third biographer of the VP, and his dramatic conversion to Clairvaux. Bernard is depressed as he passes through Paris, having been prevailed upon to preach at the School, but the call to men to forsake all does not go unheeded in that intellectual climate, and he is rewarded with a fine catch!

Fragmenta, 9
On hearing the 'mellifluous doctor' preach (a legendary phrase in Bernardine scholarship) at the School of Paris, Geoffrey arose instantly to follow Bernard as a devoted disciple, leaving his studies at the feet of his master, Peter Abelard. He waxes lyrically on that moment of spiritual awakening, dwelling on the inestimable change wrought upon his soul by God when he was

> *a man exceedingly contrary and perverse, [and] making another man of me, the embryonic beginnings of his creature. I shall never forget through all eternity the compassion which so bounteously forestalled me and changed me so suddenly as to leave men agape with stupefaction. There were many fish caught in the Lord's net in that haul, and more joined up with us on the road, so that after the probationary year there were twenty-one of our company professed.* (Matarasso, 1993: 41)

This is the heart of monastic renewal: converts become followers and their friends follow them so that the friendship circle expands in ever-increasing number. Restoration of the soul to God is the electrical charge to bring restitution to the circuit of the body corpus— monasticism reformed by the friendship of like-minded sparky sojourners! The spillover of *joie de vivre* in friendships in the public square has taken us from the wide world of high ecclesiastical office to the smaller world of monastic communities. We turn now to the centre of the action, to the heart of the power for change, to the idea of Bernard as God's friend in society.

BERNARD AS GOD'S FRIEND IN SOCIETY

It is common parlance that with every great man there is a dark side, a downside, a side which, in retrospect, does not make sense. We begin with a negative, with an enterprise which seems less to embody friendship with God and more to embolden Bernard himself by virtue of its formidable force. Formerly a knight of a military aristocracy, whose hereditary right to feud is mere bread and butter, the jump to knight for Christ is easily made. Jumping on board an Italian political campaign to send reinforcements to the East, to prosperous and strategic Byzantium besieged by the Turk; the carrot is the Muslim encroachment on Jerusalem: the Holy City, the centre of the earth, the mystical union of heaven and earth, and the place of pilgrimage.

A crusading passion to take back the Holy Land from the Infidel stirred up martial zeal and Christian ideal, and of the new military orders, the Templars (founded 1119) most epitomised an order of monks-in-arms. They swore to live according to the Benedictine rule by taking vows of poverty, chastity and obedience, and to 'fight with pure mind for the supreme and true King' (Keen, 1968: 122). The simple robe of white, symbolising purity and emblazoned with the red cross of the Crusaders, was of the same colour as that of the Cistercians, uniting monastic austerity and the spirit of chivalry found in the romance of Galahad and the Holy Grail (Keen, 1998: 122).

Brian Patrick McGuire, Professor Emeritus at Roskilde University, summarises the findings of scholarship on the controversial and questionable matter of Bernard's preaching and endorsement of the Second Crusade (1147–1150). McGuire (2020: 277–282) reinforces the generally accepted view that, at the instruction of Pope Eugenius III, and despite his frail health, Bernard willingly committed himself to preaching the necessity of another crusade, holding dear the defence of the Jerusalem of his Lord, an operation to be strengthened by French Crusaders. The entry of Saladin the Turk into Jerusalem heralded the failure of the Crusade and the end of a dream of a Frankish state in the East. Bernard's nationalist and fundamentalist Christianity is a sign, not only of his times, but of the xenophobic trends of our day. Although Bernard did not advocate war, he cannot be seen as a passivist, believing that a military victory would lead to the conversion of an entire race to the Faith. In this he was morally bright with charismatic chutzpa but incapable of uniting the French and German kings, the Knights Templar, and the Byzantine emperor in a common cause. He simply had not the political nous nor secular clout to handle the complexities of culture and context.

TRUTH-TELLING

From this intrepid incursion into the tenuous world of political drama by a mature yet ephemeral Bernard, to the concrete reality of the monastic perch from which he sang—his voice vibrating with a timbre known only to the intimates of God. What does

IN SEARCH OF FRIENDSHIP

the indefatigable lover of Jesus have to say to the consciences of leaders, both secular and spiritual alike? A detailed explanation of the convoluted and tumultuous period of division in the Western Church, caused by two men each claiming to be pope, is unnecessary for the purposes of this chapter. What is of interest is Bernard's great vigour and expertise with which he tackled and interacted with councils, city leaders and ecclesiastics by means of visits and letters. He is a political strategist functioning outside the walls of the monastery with urban and secular leaders as he tries to unify the Italian city states under the true pope, Innocent II. These efforts are successful and the anti-pope Anacletus II is finally vanquished.

Letter 129

Bernard's exploits in the papal schism of 1130–1138 are as much a call to arms as were the crusades. He comes out fighting from his cell: a contemplative in action, in what may be seen as a new development in monasticism. It marks the development, too, of Bernard's entry into the public square, a moment noted by Elder (2011: 115): 'After his eloquent, and persuasive, defence of Innocent II in the Anacletan schism in the early 1130s, Bernard had become a public figure, always on the road in defence of the reform Church.' A letter to the bishops of Aquitane (1131) shows Bernard in full stride as God's conscience, he himself 'devoured by zeal for the house of God' [Psa. 69:9] the provocative words he uses with which to cajole and wheedle the prelates. Choose Innocent, banish Anacletus:

> *The time has come, most reverend and holy fathers, for you to take courage, if you have any, and bestir yourselves to action. Once more the sword of the enemy seems to be threatening death to the whole body of Christ, but it is at you that it is being especially pointed, it is over you especially that it is being wheeled [sic]. You have the choice of either strongly resisting these daily attacks upon you or of shamefully yielding to them… The question is this: which of these two men seems to be the Pope? There is a great difference between the two persons but, so as not to seem*

> to flatter or abuse either, I will see what you will find being said
> everywhere and what I do not think anyone will deny, namely that
> the character and good name of Innocent need fear no comparison
> with that of his adversary, while his is not safe even amongst his
> friends. Then if you examine the elections you will at once see
> that ours is more honest, more creditable, and the first in time…
> It must be clear, most reverend and illustrious fathers, that it is a
> solemn duty to resist with all our might this malicious, unworthy,
> and rash effort. This is a matter that concerns every child of
> God, but it especially concerns you and yours, if you are really
> devoured by zeal for the house of God. (Le 129.1,13,14: 191,198)

Letter 147

The death of Anacletus the anti-pope in 1138 brought a welcome end to the papal schism. To celebrate the sweet taste of victory, Bernard sings a melodious and harmonious paean of praise to his friend and oft-opponent the black-robed Cluniac abbot, Peter, which expresses the joy they have in their friendship and offers thanksgiving for the triumph. The epistle seems to have been written while Bernard is away from Clairvaux; it mentions being 'among strangers' and the hopefulness of a visit to Cluny on the way back home. Here is another of those important journeys beyond the monastery so frowned upon by the Rule.

The salutation is loving and friendly, Bernard giving to Peter 'the entire devotion of his heart.' The letter begins with a reminder of Peter's vulnerability as he exposes his soul to his friend in a previous letter:

> In your letter, that letter wherein you have poured forth your
> soul to me, I have something to be proud of amongst strangers. I
> am proud to think you keep me, not only in memory, but also in
> favour. I am proud to enjoy the privilege of your affection, and I
> am refreshed by the great goodness of your heart. I am also proud
> of my troubles, if I may be counted worthy to suffer them for the
> sake of the church. But most of all it is the triumph of the Church

IN SEARCH OF FRIENDSHIP

> *of which I am proud and which keeps my head erect. If we have shared in her labours, so also shall we share in her consolation... I give thanks to God who has given her victory... The time is approaching for me to return to my brethren and, if I should live to do so I hope to visit you on my way back.* (Le 147.1, 2: 216)

As God's heavenly friend on earth, Bernard can be a double-edged sword, quite capable of being opponent and friend at the same time. He is able to straddle the median way and to keep his friends close to his heart while ticking them off for their actions or conduct. In the extract from Letter 147 above, Bernard writes wearing the hat of friendship. In Letter 179 he wears the hat of judge of his friend's deeds. Although the ecclesiastical fracas of Letter 179 is a most important affair of church government and not a mere petty quarrel of a trivial personal nature, it is precisely the loving intimacy of the friendship which is upheld despite their differences. He and Peter may be on opposite sides of church reform at times, as we see from Letter 179, but in Letter 147 Bernard consolidates their friendship and alliance. He is an ambassador of reconciliation (cf. 2 Cor. 5:20) when it counts, and Cluny is a significant project on his reforming radar.

Letter 179

The date is 1136, the papal schism furore is in full flow and Bernard's account of events is a detailed narration (Le 179.1–5: 249–52). Abbot Peter's elected candidate for Bishop of Langres flares into a quarrel, certain religious persons of the reform party try to persuade Bernard to contest it and stand for election. When this news reaches Bernard he is travelling, on his way back to Clairvaux 'tired and ill'. He finds the inner motivation to take a stand on the matter for the sake of truth, sending his own messenger to intervene and prevent the consecration of the said elected candidate. Miraculously, the ceremony is arrested, the the plan thwarted.

Circumventing Peter and any other ecclesiastical dignitaries, Bernard goes straight to the top and writes to Innocent II as 'his' pope—an attentive and ample recipient of a straightforward, logical, and honest report of these capricious circumstances. The choice of candidate is plainly one whom the local gentry favour, the kowtowing by the archbishop politically posturing so as not to rock the boat: 'All that I have said is the very truth and no lie. The truth itself shall be my witness that I have said nothing out of personal hatred but, solely for the love of truth, have stated the facts as they stand' (Le 179.5: 252). Bernard firmly believes that he is on the side of truth in this matter.

Such is the power of Bernard's hidden sleight of hand that the catastrophe is averted and a Cistercian, the prior Geoffrey of Clairvaux is elected to the hotly contested post. The charismatic 46-year-old Bernard has no qualms about supporting his own monk and thereby securing the future progress of their movement. This was not an isolated incident; procuring bishoprics for his Cistercian monks occurred on other occasions. Today we might question such interference, labelling this preferential option as medieval cronyism. The immense attractiveness of Bernard, his simplicity and fervour were a winning force which broke through the barricade of secular churchmanship, elbowing those perceived as unspiritual persons out of the way. A monastic reformer at heart; a hybrid monk-cum-churchman by expression. He would agree with the Apostle Paul: 'We have no power to act against the truth, but only for it' (2 Cor. 13:9).

Letter 51

God's man finds himself in demand and he is recruited by a reforming party seeking to rid the Church of the felony of simony, i.e. the purchase of church office or position. The fact that Bernard is a successful spokesperson and leader in these campaigns does not exempt him from criticism: a monk, in truth an abbot cannot neglect abbatial duties and run after councils and controversies. Petty jealousies of the narrow-minded plague Bernard, who writes to the papal chancellor, Cardinal Haimeric in self-defence of his input at the council of Châlons-sur-Marne (1129) complaining that he has been 'dragged' into these controversies against his will. Bernard is at his most ironic in this letter, expressing pleasure that the cardinal is 'displeased'. His language is fulsome as he begs the cardinal to command the 'noisy and importunate frogs' (the croaking of his opponents) to keep to their domestic domains and to leave him in peace:

> Cannot wretchedness escape envy? Must truth breed hatred even for the poor and needy? Should I be glad or should I deplore that I am treated as an enemy? Is it because I spoke the truth or because I did right?... I was present, I do not deny it. But I was summoned and dragged there... I am vexed at having been embroiled in these disputes, especially as I knew that I was not concerned personally in them. I am vexed, but I am dragged into them none the less... I am delighted to know that you are displeased that I should have been concerned in these affairs. It is most just and friendly of you. May it please you to bestir yourself in the matter, and because you understand that it is expedient for your friend and becoming for a monk, see that what we both want is speedily effected and for the salvation of my soul. May it please you to bid the noisy and importunate frogs to keep their holes and remain contented with their ponds. See that they are heard no more in the councils of the mighty or seen in the palaces of the great for the sake of justice and for the salvation of my soul. (Le 51.1–3: 79–81)

Despite Bernard's protestations at having been 'dragged' into the council, the fact remains that he seemed pleased to have been asked and proved a formidable opponent, exactly what the Church reformers needed. He may even have perceived of his role as prophetic, as acting for God as an agent of change, of being God's mouthpiece. Certainly, this is the case if one is of the opinion that leadership in the twelfth century is largely charismatic and prophetic (Sommerfeldt, 1991: xiv).

DECISION-MAKING

To be God's friend in society is to march to the beat of a different drum. For Bernard, a contemplative monk does not disengage his mind when he is coming to a decision. A contemplative monk is not so wrapped up in his prayer cell in faraway dreams that he cannot seize love and truth and relate them to everyday issues. This is common-sense reflection. We return to the treatise *On Consideration*, written to a person in power, Pope Eugenius III, as a response to the failure of the Second Crusade. Bernard is distressed and wishes to make sense of an enterprise which he had inspired, even instructed to call by Eugenius. What had gone wrong? He concludes that the fault lay in the Crusaders, the pilgrims whose hearts were not true. These remarks must lead us to conclude that, despite his weaknesses, Bernard is committed to truth and to learning from mistakes. His naivety in attributing the failure of the Second Crusade to a lack of purity on the part of the Crusaders merely illustrates his simplicity of heart and his single-minded vision when it came to the expansion of the Gospel.

We left the inquiry in an earlier section at Book 5 with a reminder that a leader ought to act and speak keeping an eternal perspective in mind. An inspection of Bernard's method in solving and resolving the trickier issues takes us to his thinking in Book 2 around the spiritual practices of contemplation and consideration and their separation into two habits to be cultivated—an idea which will be examined more closely in Chapter 4.

On Consideration

We may understand the difference between the two disciplines thus: contemplation is an interior position, whereby the soul receives by faith and without doubt the truth known without logic and intuitively to the mind; whereas consideration is a mode of wrestling with a matter in the mind in order to grasp the truth of something. Contemplation may be viewed as a passive action; consideration as an active *modus operandi*. Evans observes that contemplation is 'the true and sure perception of the mind, an apprehension of truth in which there is no doubt'; consideration, on the other hand, 'is searching for truth, active thinking and balancing and judging' (1987: 145).

Bernard defines contemplation and consideration as marked by a specific characteristic pertaining to what is known and what is unknown:

> First of all, consider what it is I call consideration. For I do not want it to be understood as entirely synonymous with contemplation, because the latter concerns more what is known about something while consideration pertains more to the investigation of what is unknown. Consequently, contemplation can be defined as the true and sure intuition of the mind concerning something, or the apprehension of truth without doubt. Consideration, on the other hand, can be defined as thought searching for truth, or the searching of a mind to discover truth. (Csi 2.2.5: 52)

There are four things to take into account in order to reap the reward of consideration and they are presented in a sequence: 'yourself, what is below you, around you and above you' (2.3.6: 52). The first, that of knowing oneself and considering oneself, is vital as it locates the person right at the centre of the thinking process, thereby saving it from mere theoretical speculation. Being ignorant of the inner self will lead to outward aspirations which are constructed in materials of dust:

> Your consideration should begin with yourself so you do not reach out to other things in vain, because you have neglected yourself. What does it profit you if you gain the whole world and lose one person—yourself? [cf. Matt. 16:26]... if you do not know yourself, you are like a building without a foundation; you raise not a structure but ruins [cf. Luke 6:49]. Whatever you construct outside yourself will be but a pile of dust blown by the wind... let your consideration begin and end with yourself. (2.3.6: 53)

And beginning with the self means that the precise nature of consideration is tested by the integrity of the words spoken; they must be gathered as part of the salvation of one's soul and, therefore, be seen as contributing to one's personal salvation. Speak with care, as what you say reflects the state of your saved soul. Test your words:

> Your word is your consideration; if it proceeds, let it not withdraw... You must reject anything which presents itself for your consideration that does not pertain in some way to your salvation. (2.3.6: 53)

Any consideration of the self should be around three components: what you are in nature e.g. a man; who you are in person e.g. a pope; what sort of person you are in character e.g. kind, friendly, gentle etc. (2.4.7: 54). With these three things in mind, Bernard is not afraid to go where angels fear to tread: to keep a pope in high office in constant remembrance of himself, who he is, who he was and who he must be: his lowly calling, his first call to be monk, his responsibility in being a friend of God:

> Now we must turn our attention to who you are now and who you were before you were made pope... You have not forgotten your first profession: what is out of reach is not out of mind or at least has not left your heart. Your commands, your judgments and your teachings will benefit if you do not lose sight of that profession. This consideration makes you scorn honours in the midst of honours... High position is not designed to flatter, for it involves greater responsibility. High position threatens danger; responsibility is the proof of a friend. (2.5.8: 55–56)

Bernard is a first-rate coach in that he is not intimidated by the status of Eugenius. He sees him for what he is: a professed monk given higher responsibility who must take good care of his soul if he is to execute his duties in a godly, not a worldly, way. Consideration is not contemplation and herein lies its uniqueness when applied especially to leadership. The heart of the matter is the quest for truth, which in our age of fake news and relativity seems peculiarly apt when considering the task of leading with integrity.

If these considerations have engaged with the self, the first of the four elements listed above, and previously addressed above in the realm of God, it is important not to neglect the middle two components viz. what is below (treatment of subordinates) and what is around (the position in the world at large), an elaboration of which comprises the substance of Books 2, 3 and 4.

Evans pinpoints the significance of Bernard's declaration: 'a view of papal plenitude of power and of the supremacy of spiritual over temporal power that was to be enormously influential in the later Middle Ages, continuing as it did the direction of the changes of the late eleventh century.' (1987: 145). In summary: The Pope's spiritual authority is huge and greater than emperor or king. But the Pope is not a private person, he is a public person, the representative of worlds. With this in mind portions of Bernard's manual for decision-making are written along the lines of stewardship over the earth, not possession:

> So also, you should preside in order to provide, to counsel, to administer, and to serve. Preside so as to be useful; preside so as to be the faithful and prudent servant whom the Lord has set up over his family. For what purpose? So you may give them their food in due season; that is, so that you may administer, not rule ... there is no poison more dangerous for you, no sword more deadly, than the passion to rule. (3.2.2: 80–81)

In truth, these set of instructions could well be applied to Christian leadership in general as the Gospels tell us not to lord it over one another as the people of this world, but to serve (Matt. 20:25; Mark 10:42-45).

GOD-HONOURING

The way of the servant is the way of obedience and right living so that society is impacted and changed. In his life and works Bernard is an exemplar of the biblical principle of being salt and light in society (Matt. 5:13–16). His emergence from the enclave of the monastery to speak and act in the wider community brings with it a strong witness to Jesus Christ. He cannot help himself: his tireless devotion and desire for God is an unflagging zeal for the honour of God. And what better way to honour God than in a return to the true virtues of the monastic call?

Father Michael Casey, OCSO (Order of the Cistercians of Strict Observance) is a Trappist monk of the Tarrawarra Abbey in Australia, and, therefore, a good analyst of Bernard who became identified with Cistercian reform. In calibrating the message of Bernard, Casey makes a worthwhile and noteworthy argument for his preaching, teaching, and living out the Rule of Benedict according to its authentic meaning, values which he internalised and brilliantly expounded (2011: 97). It is the very rigour, austerity, and hardship which he espoused which drew his recruits, especially from among the vigorous and high-minded. And these same monastic ideals are projected on to secular society so that he became its social critic (Casey, 2011: 98). To Henry of Sens Bernard writes: 'These are the insignia of the monk: hard work, the hidden life and voluntary poverty' (Ep.42.37; SBO 7:130.21–22, trans. Casey, 2011: 98).

Letter 151

To the monks of the abbey in the Alps in the diocese of Geneva, St. Jean-d'Aulps, which becomes an affiliate of Clairvaux, Bernard writes, dwelling on the elevation to a high place of their abbot to bishop in contrast to the status of the gathered monks and stressing the virtues of the Benedictine Rule:

> *Our place is the bottom, is humility, is voluntary poverty,*
> *obedience, and joy in the Holy Spirit. Our place is under a master,*
> *under an Abbot, under a rule, under discipline. Our place is*
> *to cultivate silence, to exert ourselves in fasts, vigils, prayers,*
> *manual work and, above all, to keep that 'more excellent way'*

IN SEARCH OF FRIENDSHIP

> which is the way of charity; and furthermore to advance day by
> day in these things, and to persevere in them until the last day.
> I trust that this is what you are busily doing. (Le 151.1: 220)

Bernard loves the humility of the monks, a virtue which he rates more highly than ascetic practices, word of which has gone forth from the abbey to the outside world:

> You have proved yourselves truly humble by this judging
> yourselves unprofitable servants. It is so rare that anyone leading
> a good life is ready to do this that when it happens everyone
> admires it... wherever word of your action has gone abroad,
> it has filled everything with the fragrance of its sweetness.
> In my opinion this virtue is to be preferred to long fasts and
> protracted vigils, in fact to every bodily exercise. (2: 220)

Bernard as Father Abbot of the entire Cistercian Order throws open his arms to these steadfast, and likeable brethren, as do the shining throng of celestial beings:

> The Cistercian multitude welcomed you with open arms, and
> the angels looked down upon you with smiling faces. (2: 220)

The great joy with which his little flock at Clairvaux receives these newly joined brethren is a matter for more wonderful words:

> I cannot describe how great and special is the love with which they
> welcome you. No words can express the mutual charity which
> the Holy Spirit has marvellously inspired between us. (3: 220)

Now it remains for these blessed brothers to seek a new abbot, a new father in God. To wait for Bernard to return to them will take too long—knowing his busy schedule—Godfrey Prior of Clairvaux will be sent, or at least one whom he will send in his place, to help this process:

> It now remains for you, my brothers, to invoke the Holy
> Spirit and set about electing your father. (3: 220–221)

The testimony of Isaac of Stella

Little is known of Isaac of Stella born in about 1100 in England, attracted to the Schools in France and quite possibly a pupil of Abelard. As Abbot of Stella in his thirties he sought a greater solitude and austerity. He knew and had met Bernard and wrote of him with capacious appreciation (Matarasso, 1993: 201). In a beautifully crafted piece, Isaac writes of Bernard's overwhelming attractiveness, quoted in full to help get a sense of the measure of the man as this section on a God-honouring friend is brought to a close:

> We have seen a man that had something superhuman. His actions and rebukes have in his absence caused some whom he scorched to murmur against him. But, in his features there was a sort of divine majesty, inducing at once both peace and fear yet worthy of love and the respect of charity. Grace was poured out on his lips, and anointed his face to reproach those who reproached him so that they came to love, praise and proclaim all that he did… we are speaking of holy Bernard, abbot of Clairvaux. In his absence he seemed like the sun and the moon and a fearsome army, but when he was present he always flowed with delights so that though his love was demanding, his demands were lovable. In his speaking or in imposing discipline, he never let others become discouraged by pusillanimity or to burn with impatience or to become a victim to envy. (Isaac of Stella, *Sermons* 52.15; Sources chrétiennes, 339, 1987: 234, trans. Casey, 2011: 82)

Isaac singles out the five virtues which acted like a magnet upon people, drawing them towards God and the inner workings of his grace: innocent and without malice; munificent in generosity to others and concern for their welfare; enthusiastic in word and deed and extremely wide awake; influential in his holiness; and, loving and lovable (Casey, 2011: 83). In other words, Bernard lived what he preached and was, in the words of Paul a 'living letter', an epistle to be read by all (2 Cor.3:2–3).

Isaac of Stella's Third Sermon for the Feast of Pentecost has a depiction of the Holy Spirit at work in creation and in the individual soul. This is the strength of Bernard and the source of his power, which rouses men and women from sluggishness and apathy to contemplate and honour God:

> [S]o does the Holy Spirit move over the spiritual waters, a kind of mediator between the sluggishness below and the steel of heaven's justice, protecting and cherishing them, and quickening them with his love and grace, lest they be utterly consumed and the earth crack open with drought. (trans. Matarasso: 210)

As a light in society, Bernard shone with a brilliance and luminosity, outshining all other lights in the firmament. As salt in the cracks of the fabric of a drought-ridden society, his words brought chastisement, sorrow, and transformation. As a mouthpiece for God he could be brutal and life-giving at the same time. As one who held others to account, he was tenacious and obstinate. As McGuire—one among other historians and scholars—has elegantly opined, Bernard is 'a difficult saint' (2020: 1). It is not our business to encapsulate his legacy, merely to extract lessons to be learned from it. As a friend in high places he attempted to keep the power brokers accountable to God. As a friend in low places he loved and cajoled.

Chapter 4

FRIENDSHIP IN THE CIRCLE OF ETERNAL LOVE

'Isn't it odd. We can only see our outsides,
but nearly everything happens on the inside.'

We have come to see that the luminosity of Bernard both attracted and repelled: the searchlight of his inspiring spirituality probed the darkness and shadows as a laser beam, exposing sin and corruption, and the brightness of its beam cast its radiant arc around Europe as a prophetic declaration of love in hard times. Love must act justly and keep the commandment in word and deed. He feeds the common people still struggling for the daily crust at the gates of the abbey, hundreds of peasants each day. His words ring out as revolution, a protest at the magnificence of the many monastic and church buildings throughout the country:

> The church shines with splendour on all sides, but the poor are hungry... The walls of the church are covered with gold, but the children of the church go naked... Ah Lord! If the folly of it all does not shame us, surely the expense might stick in our throats?... You will seal my lips saying that it is not for a monk to judge,

> *please God that you seal my eyes also so that I may not see. But if I hold my peace, the poor, the naked, and the starving would cry out.* (Trans. Clegg et al. cited in Leroux-Dhuys, 1998: 34)

Bernard is not a pushover. He demands excellence and purity. Bernard is no plaster saint: he is *in via*, on the move toward God, and the more he loves God, the more his influence is extended. And we who have embarked on a journey to understand the man and his times are not are not merely to plumb his meaning but more directly and purposefully to know his heart. From whence does his passion derive its drive and how does his interior life evolve? How is he able to maintain a posture of stern friendship and amiability simultaneously? How is he capable of holding friendships lightly in the monastery, whilst travelling outside the walls of its enclosure, the confidant of the rich and powerful? How does he keep the bonds of love and affection strong and, more than that, continue to grow and develop as a human being? In our search for answers we must come to terms with the way in which his spiritual life is formed and developed.

This chapter is in three parts: Bernard on formation in the love of God; Bernard on friendship as formation in the love of God; and, Bernard on formation within the fellowship of divine love. The chapter is organised along lines which bring us back to the beginning in a perpetual circle of divine love in motion. We start at any point on this circle's circumference and it will always bring us back to God, the Alpha and Omega, the beginning and end. In medieval thought, the circle may represent God who is round, for the Father is eternity and the Trinity is completely perfect and ceaselessly moving like a wheel (*Hildegard Bingensis* Ep.312: 12–21 van Acker and Klaes-Hachmöller, in Campbell, 2012: 69). Wherever we begin in the circle of human love and friendship in Bernard, it is always in and through and by means of God, who is love. All friendship, all love, is caught and captured and held prisoner to that greater love.

Formation, therefore, in the Bernadine way. An abbot seasoned in the spiritual disciplines, but we are not concerned with lists and tick boxes—a mechanical method of achieving spiritual composure—but with the man as a whole person, whose inner disposition is centred on love for Jesus above all else. We begin with one or two remarks on the *Amplexus*, the unusual depiction of Bernard's affection for Jesus, perhaps, to our contemporary sensibilities, an outlandish and mythically primitive occurrence.

The *Amplexus*

For medieval people quite at home with visual expressions of devotion, their favourite saints shown in murals or statuary in postures of worship, Bernard's embrace (*amplexus*) by Christ would be not only perfectly appropriate but compelling and persuasive. To see Bernard with the arms of Jesus around him is exactly how his piety is perceived at the time by peasant and nobleman alike, whether the story is true, or not. The first popular representation, and the only one truly original, is the *Amplexus Bernardi*, which is the pictorial equivalent of a scene from a popular tale of Christ bent down from the cross to embrace Bernard kneeling before him. Bernard is identified in this way in the popular imagination, as much as in the traditional attributes of book, cowl and crozier the signs and symbols of saint, monk, and abbot respectively (France, 2011: 325). And what is it about this narrative which is off-putting for moderns? Here is Bernard in much the same way as people today speak of having seen the Lord or encountered him directly by way of vision or dream. The slight difference being that there is an observer, allegedly, watching the saint at prayer.

The first account is found in a collection called *Liber Miraculorum* (Book of Miracles) assembled by Herbert of Clairvaux toward the end of the twelfth century and included in the *Exordium magnum* by Conrad of Eberbach in the early thirteenth century (France, 2011: 325). Menard, a former abbot of Mores tells how a monk, presumably himself, is a witness to an extraordinary event, believable because, for the narrator, Bernard is 'beyond the human condition' and elevated to a higher plane (cf. Paul's vision of the third heaven, 2 Cor. 12:2).

IN SEARCH OF FRIENDSHIP

> *I heard of a certain monk who had once found the blessed abbot Bernard alone in church deep in prayer prostrate before the altar, a cross with its crucified appeared placed on the floor in front of him. This the most blessed man devoutly adored and kissed. Then that Majesty removed his arms from the branches of the cross and he seemed to embrace the servant of God and draw him to himself.* (Exordium magnum 2.20, ed. Griesser, cited in France, 2011: 325–326)

We may never know the authenticity of this record, but such was its impact that it was handed down from one century to the next as epitomising Bernardine devotion. The significant features which stand out are firstly, the bodily embrace, and secondly, the intimacy of the contact. These two outstanding factors mark out Bernard's approach to worship. The body is not separate in the offering of the self to God. Quite the contrary, the body as a physical entity is joined to the soul in adoration. Thus, the entire being, the body and the soul, is at worship, stretched out, prostrated before the crucified Christ. And the God-man before him is himself in bodily form, cruciform and in the shape of the cross: Jesus incarnate. Divine body to human body in an embrace of love, the cleaving to one another so that the two become one. The closeness of togetherness in a clasp of unity is the soul seeking union with the divine. The intimacy initiated by God coming toward the figure on the floor.

Bernard preaches to his brothers on this theme, the Latin text from which he worked better able to translate his meaning than contemporary translations: *mihi autem adhēreō Deo bonum est*, 'For me it is good to cleave to God' (Psa. 72:28), *adhēreō* with the meaning to cleave, to cling to, to attach. (cp. 'But my chief good is to be near you, God' Psa. 73:28 NRSV). He tells them:

> Good indeed, if you cleave wholly to him. Who is there who cleaves perfectly to God, unless he who, dwelling in God, is loved by God and, reciprocating that love, draws God into himself. Therefore, when God and man cleave wholly to each other—it is when they are

incorporated into each other by mutual love that they cleave wholly to each other—I would say beyond all doubt that God is in man and man is in God. (SS 71.4.10, trans. Edmonds, 1980, 4: 56–57)

We may compare and contrast the posture of the Bernardine lover of Christ with that of the twentieth-century graphic embodiment in sculpture of a wrestling Jacob at the River Jabbok (Gen. 32:22-32). Jacob Epstein's monumental group—a human and a divine messenger, or God—shows the two colossal figures locked in a nightlong struggle: the tight embrace, the limp surrender of the man held up by the stronger winner (tate.org.uk/art/artworks/epstein-jacob-and-the-angel-t07139).

The narrative in both may be similar in the soul's search for meaning and love, but the way of attainment is at odds: passivity and yearning desire in the account older by 800 years, active pressing challenge in the contemporary interpretation. Perhaps a snapshot of the two contrasting eras: the medieval acceptance of the lordship of the Saviour, the post-Enlightenment modern battle with deity.

Yet in both, there is that sense of timelessness, of the divine-human relationship needing to be articulated and, in some strange sense, wordless in the embrace. Dorothy Sölle remarks that in a mystical or poetic text there is the possibility of not only naming or calling the silence, but of producing it, of being able to create an expanse between speech and speechlessness, of a silent cry against an institution governed by regularity and order (2001: 45, 71, 72). We see this stance in Bernard's writings and life: a lone solitary in reforming mode, modelling a way of life as a pattern for others to follow; fashioned himself by a masterly hand, certainly the Rule but ordered by the Lover and his school of love.

BERNARD ON FORMATION IN THE LOVE OF GOD

Bernard is a contemplative writing at a leisurely pace without thought of time. He is not hidebound by our age and its desire to conquer worlds and words in an instant. He is a poet and writes as a medieval, throwing out food for thought and reflection. As a thinker and observer of his own time Bernard is remarkably close to our own. The temptations, despairs, pains, and anxieties which are so much a part of our lives today are an echo of his age. In some ways he may even be viewed as a forerunner to our modern and postmodern absorption with the self, although his analysis never reached our sophisticated heights. His remedy for the self's shortcomings was very simply: God. Leclercq pinpoints the measure of the man as commensurate with self-knowledge through experience (1987: 31). For Bernard, experience leads to reflection on one's unique history in the light of God's grace and his word, on one's pitiable condition apart from God, which sends one back to God to an experience of his love and to serve the brothers according to that love. Leclercq puts it thus:

> *The point of departure for Bernard's entire doctrine is an intense, personal experience of the interior struggle. All of his theology is merely a reflection on this primary fact in light of the Gospels and St Paul. He reflected on it daily, recognising that it was also the experience of every man.* (1987: 36)

AWARENESS OF THE SELF

Love is the beginning and end of all Bernard's thinking and the realisation of that love in human experience is his goal as he writes and speaks. Union with God in a mystical sense, those sublime moments of bliss (the example of the *amplexus* comes to mind) is given at a price and is the consequence, for Bernard, of denial of the body in ascetic practices. Love leads to God and loving God with all one's being starts with the body which, for Bernard, is a good thing (again, the surrender of the body in the *amplexus*). To discipline the body, to control the appetites is to recall the body to its purpose for God. As Leclercq points out, Bernard's belief that the libido can be sublimated resonates with modern ideas, as does his value given to human desire (1987: 41–42).

The body

However, despite this psychological slant, and almost because of it, we cannot get away from the fact that Bernard's anthropology is, essentially, monastic. We cannot dress him up in fashionable psychosomatic garb when it come to the body. His relationship with the body is slightly more complex than this. Sommerfeldt admirably draws out the distinctions: Bernard is at one and the same time hostile to the body in its carnality, affirming of the body in that God used the body to draw his creatures to himself in the incarnation, and yet ambivalent to the body as being of the earth and to be transcended by things spiritual (1991: 3–4). An extract from a sermon for the Ascension has the preacher speaking with two voices. The first is for the body as a vehicle for the Lord's presence on earth. By means of beautiful imagery, Bernard conjures up the incarnation of the Son of God, an adjustment to the physical body of humankind so as to show the brightness of the glory of God:

> *The Lord of the apostles presented himself to the apostles in such a way that they would no longer perceive the invisible things of God as understood by the things that are made, but that the very Maker of all things would himself be seen face to face. Because the disciples were beings of flesh and God is spirit, and spirit and flesh are not easily brought together, he adapted himself to them with the shadow of his body, that by the intervention of his life-giving flesh they might behold the Word in flesh, the sun in a cloud, light in an earthen jug, the candle in the lantern.* (SSS 3.3, trans. Kienzle, 1991: 38)

The second voice is against the body as that which is inferior to the spirit, but the Lord uses the body, in which resides the spirit, and from whom comes the miraculous and the life of God to incline the affections of human beings to himself:

> For this purpose [the Lord] set his flesh before them, to turn their every thought away from human matters and attach it to his flesh, which was saying wondrous things and performing wondrous deeds. Thus he would turn [their] attention from flesh to spirit, because 'God is spirit, and those who worship God must worship in spirit and in truth.' (SSS 3.3, 1991: 39)

Bernard's philosophy of the body is pragmatic. We are 'bodily creatures', carnal and sold under sin. We must be reorientated to God. The process of conversion to God, therefore, begins with the flesh in cooperation with the will: 'it is unavoidable that our desire and love should begin with the body and if it is rightly directed, it will then proceed by grace through certain stages, until the spirit it fulfilled' (LG 15.39: 204). The drives of human nature will result in 'bodily love, by which man loves himself for his own sake' (LG 8.23: 192). The body must be ordered toward its proper end, love for God and neighbour and for this reason at times is to be denied what it desires and restrained to turn away from pleasures and be content with the right amounts of food and clothing:

> Then will your love be sober and just, when you do not deny your brother what he needs from the pleasures you have denied yourself. It is in this way that bodily love is shared, when it is extended to the community. (LG 8.23: 192)

The outworking of the principle of shared 'bodily love' at Clairvaux is shown by Geoffrey of Auxerre in an encomium preached on the tenth anniversary of Bernard's death (*Sermo in anniversario obitus S. Bernardi* 10–11, trans. Casey, 2011: 79–81). He highlights his Abbot's gift of bringing healing to the wounded soul, of coming alongside others to weep or rejoice with them, of his care for the sick, of his personal interest in his monks, cautioning the strong against sloth,

FRIENDSHIP IN THE CIRCLE OF ETERNAL LOVE

the fervent to take rest (10: 79). Bernard had an intimate knowledge of his community and its needs.

> It was easy for him to perceive what was troubling anyone because he was very familiar with what went on inside each monk. He made provision for each with great kindness in case one should be weighed down with too much work or another corrupted by too much quiet. It was as though he took a personal interest in how much sleep they all got. (11: 80)

Geoffrey tells how an unfair burden was never put upon the brothers and how each was helped in their carrying the yoke of Christ more easily. Bernard would say:

> 'This one is cold. This one has a lot on his mind. This one is working too hard. The food is not right for this one. Here is one who has been hurt by another. One has to bear a heavy burden; not less a burden is borne by another who feels that he has been hurt. It is of great importance to bring grace to those who are offended.' (11: 80)

Geoffrey's praise is for one who was himself not always in the best of health and yet cared and cured his brothers.

> What is surprising is that one man could simultaneously accomplish all these functions, especially one who was himself subject to a variety of ailments. Though unequal in strength, he showed himself equal to the robust and the recently arrived in fasting and vigils. Though he was sick he visited the sick. (11: 80)

The extremities to which Bernard took denial of the flesh is a dense topic which could prove a distraction from our purpose of discovering what constitutes good spiritual formation. As a young poet, visionary, and genius, he may be forgiven the punishing diet, the bouts of illnesses and the severity of his personal spiritual regime. As an older abbot, the ministrations of the brothers rescued him, correcting the imbalances. Through bodily weakness an identification with the suffering Jesus is made. Through ascetic denial of the flesh an intense connection with brotherly community is established. The wonder is in his achievement, his travel and his lasting impact despite his failing physique.

Bernard believes that the body is so much a part of the perfection of human nature that it must rejoin the soul and be freed of all mortal constraints in the final resurrection. The body will be raised to glory in its ultimate glorification, that described in the Letter to the Philippians: 'He will transfigure our humble bodies, and give them a form like that of his own glorious body' (3:20, cf. LG 5.14: 185).

The soul

To inhabit a body which practices ascetic acts of piety and performs good works almost as an automaton is never Bernard's intention. For genuine spiritual formation to take effect, the impetus for charity should flow from an overflow of the soul which knows its need of God and is held in the grip of grace. Pride and self-importance must fall to humility. Therefore, hand in glove with an acknowledgment of one's carnality (the sinful body), the first step back to God is in humility, finding out the truth about oneself, 'facing up to one's real self without flinching and turning aside', taking stock of oneself in the 'clear light of truth', discovering that one 'lives in a region where likeness to God has been forfeited', and 'groaning from the depths of a misery to which [he] can no longer remain blind' (Bernard, SS 36.4.5, trans. Walsh, 1976, 2: 177–178).

The list of disappointing traits through such self-analysis is lengthy and the monks listening to Sermon 36 might be forgiven for wilting under the holy fire of their abbot (and the mountain of hyperbole). It appears that true self-knowledge reveals to the monk

> *the burden of sin that he carries, the oppressive weight of his mortal body, the complexities of earthly cares, the corrupting influence of sensual desires; on seeing his blindness, his worldliness, his weakness, his embroilment in repeated errors; on seeing himself*

> *exposed to a thousand dangers, trembling amid a thousand fears, confused by a thousand difficulties, defenceless before a thousand suspicions, worried by a thousand needs... Let him be changed and weep, changed to mourning and sighing, changed to acceptance of the Lord.* (SS 36.4.5: 178–179)

We might begin to think that we have here a mental, emotional, and spiritual bully brandishing a morally and legally binding big stick, leaving his monks languishing in a slough of despond. However, the spiritual master of love uses himself and his own struggles as a lesson on climbing out of the pit of sin—saved by the merciful goodness and compassion of God.

> *As for me, as long as I look at myself, my eye is filled with bitterness. But if I look up and fix my eyes on the aid of the divine mercy, this happy vision of God soon tempers the bitter vision of myself... This vision of God is not a little thing. It reveals him to us as listening compassionately to our prayers, as truly kind and merciful... His very nature is to be good, to show mercy always and to spare.* (36.4.6:179)

Bernard's instruction is to turn the eyes upon God and be led from self-knowledge to knowing God. The work is done. Herein is the mystery of the image of God renewed in the soul.

> *By this kind of experience, and in this way, God makes himself known to us for our good... In this way your self-knowledge will be a step to the knowledge of God; he will become visible to you according as his image is being renewed within you.* (36.4.6:179)

Humility is the by-product of knowing oneself, of knowing God's nature, of seeing God and having a vision of God. To be saved from the self is to be saved by the glorious working of God within:

> *You can see now that each of these kinds of knowledge is so*

> *necessary for your salvation, that you cannot be saved if you lack either of them. If you lack self-knowledge you will possess neither the fear of God nor humility. And whether you may presume to be saved without the fear of God and humility, is for you to judge. (36.4.7: 179)*

Bernard's next bout with his monks the following day has a teasing tongue-in-cheek feel as he repeats the lesson:

> *I presume that there is no need today to remind you to stay awake, because I feel that the remarks I made as recently as yesterday, friendly remarks, will be enough to keep those concerned on the alert. You remember that you have agreed with me etc. (SS 37.1.1: 181)*

Bernard's view of human nature is incomplete without the recognition that he understands himself well and, therefore, knows his vocation truly. Having quelled a dissident mob in the city of Rheims, he is immediately elected archbishop, a position he refuses to accept. In his explanation to King Louis VII of France is demonstrated true humility, true self-awareness, true love for God and neighbour:

> *[Y]ou would surely not be so very anxious to promote such a wretched person as myself except for the glory of God; what other reason could you have since I am poor and destitute?... I am a timorous character, broken in body, and there only remains for me the grave, I cannot on any account 'stretch forth my hands to great works'; unfitted and unequal to such a holy office... No one is better known to me than myself, no one knows me so well as I know myself. I cannot believe against my conscience those who only see me from without and judge me only by appearances. (Le 210: 285–86)*

Nearing the end of his life and Bernard is practising what he has preached: 'Humility is the virtue by which a man recognises his own unworthiness because he really knows himself' (HUM 1.2, trans. Evans, 1987: 103). This definition is from the first of Bernard's works *De gradibus humilitatis et superbiae* (*On the Steps of Humility and Pride*), a topic with which, he lightly points out, he is *au fait*. The sticking point to love is the beam in the eye, the pride which keeps the human being subject to itself and its own ways. Here is an echo of the prodigal, the fallen son who 'came to his senses' in the pig sty of life (Luke 15:17).

> *He who wants to know the whole truth about himself must, when he has removed the beam of pride (Matt. 7: 5) which is cutting off his eye from the light, cut steps in his heart (Psa.83: 6) by which he can find himself in himself.* (HUM 4.15: 113)

Confronting sin head on is the first step out of pride:

> *Those whom truth brings to know themselves it also causes to think little of themselves. It follows inevitably that all that they used to love will now become bitter to them. Brought face to face with themselves, they are forced to see things which fills them with shame. When they are distressed to see what they are, they long to be what they are not, and fear that they will never be by their own efforts. They grieve deeply over themselves, and the only consolation they can find is to judge themselves severely.* (HUM 5.18:115)

Bruun notes that the conclusion to the tractate *De gradibus humilitatis et superbiae* (*On the Steps of Humility and Pride*) has Bernard placing his ladders of humility and pride each with their twelve steps placed vertically against a horizontal landscape, providing a structure on which to move, either up (humility) or down (pride). On the landscape there is freedom of movement and an array of opportunities for entanglements, detentions and getting lost in confusing highways and byways (2011: 254; HUM 22.57: 142).

Dastardly pride ignores senselessly our created status on the one hand or sets a higher regard upon ourselves than is warranted on the other. We are to keep the middle way, the path of humility in our dealings with ourselves. The worst kind of human straying from God is that of presumption. Knowingly and deliberately, a presumptive self seeks glory for itself in good things, stealing the glory which rightly belongs to God who created all good by his power. This is treason against God. It is the greatest sin, viz. pride (LG 2.4: 177).

> And so we should greatly fear that ignorance which makes us think less of ourselves than we should. But no less, indeed rather more, should we fear that ignorance which makes us think ourselves better than we are. This is what happens when we are deceived into thinking that some good in us originates with ourselves. (LG 2.4: 177)

Bernard has a positive attitude in his exhortation to seek the best light within the human soul, knowing that by means of free will, which originates in the Creator, the soul is to return:

> You must look for higher goods in the higher part of yourself, that is, the soul. These higher goods are dignity, knowledge, virtue. Man's dignity is his free will, which is the gift by which he is superior to the animals and even rules them (Gen. 1:26). Man's knowledge is that by which he recognises that he possesses this dignity, but that it does not originate in himself. His virtue is that by which he seeks eagerly for his Creator, and when he finds him, holds to him with all his might. (LG 2.2: 176)

Pride will struggle to surrender the will, clutch at the gift given as if owned by right:

> Yet it is difficult for anyone, once he has received from God the power to will freely, to give up his will wholly to God and not rather too will things for himself. Perhaps it is impossible. He is tempted to treat what he has been given as his own, and clutch it to himself. (LG 2.6: 178)

Humility and self-knowledge give in and reach out for love:

> On the contrary, the faithful know how utterly they stand in
> need of Jesus and him crucified (1 Cor. 2:2) They wonder at and
> reach out to that supreme love of his which passes all knowledge
> (Eph.3:19). They are ashamed not to respond to such love and
> deserving with the little they have to give. (LG 3.7: 179)

For Bernard, the secret of perfection of the soul is love. From the step of humility the will has the power to choose for or against love: of God, neighbour, and self.

We turn now to the conversion of the will. The human being has responsibility for taming the will and bending it to Christ. This is accomplished by the power of free choice. As the will is brought into unity with Christ's will love grows: free love, a free lover of God, a free and happy lover of God.

The will

A radical change of direction is initiated by the conversion of the will. The term 'conversion' is an integral element of Bernard's spiritual doctrine: 'Without the energy which conversion generates, Bernard's whole system falls. Ideally conversion would lead a man to enter a Cistercian monastery' (Casey, 2011: 103). As we draw this section on self-awareness to a close, by a brief examination of the role of the will in converting the soul, we remind ourselves that Bernard lays great emphasis on personal experience. Sermon 3 of the Song of Songs begins with a call to self-examination of the book of experience, which leads to deep repentance, beginning the process of relinquishing the will:

> Today the text we are to study is the book of our own experience.
> You must therefore turn your attention inwards, each one
> must take note of his own particular awareness of the things
> I am about to discuss. (SS 3.1, trans. Walsh, 1971: 16)

The state of mourning for sin is good. It leads to repentance at the hands of the heavenly physician. Commenting on the verse,

IN SEARCH OF FRIENDSHIP

'Daughters of Jerusalem, I am dark and lovely' (Song of Songs 1: 5), Bernard asks rhetorically of the gathered brothers the reason for the loveliness of the woman, clearly wishing them to see that the beginning of the conversion of the will is humility and confession which lead to an awakening of love and a turning to the Beloved:

> *You may ask what skill enabled her to accomplish this change, or on what grounds did she merit it? I can tell you in a few words. She wept bitterly, she sighed deeply from her heart, she sobbed with a repentance that shook her very being, till the evil that inflamed her passions was cleansed away. The heavenly physician came with speed to her aid, 'because his word runs swiftly.' Perhaps you think the Word of God is not a medicine? Surely it is, a medicine strong and pungent, testing the mind and the heart… 'Awake, awake, captive daughter of Sion, awake, shake off the dust.'* (SS 3.2: 17–18)

Repentance leads the soul to see its separation from God and the futility of the past years:

> *[L]et blushes suffuse my cheeks, shame cover them like a cloud. Let my life be worn out with sorrow, my years with sights. O shame! What harvest have I gathered from deeds that now humiliate me?* (SS 16.4–5 (trans. Walsh, 1971:118)

Bernard does not let the soul off the hook by subsuming human nature under a comfort blanket of God's kindness. God is omnipotent, all-powerful, and just. To spurn God or consider him less than he is, the Maker of all things, is not to fear him and, for Bernard, a healthy fear can be a prerequisite for converting the soul. A new convert may find an unhealthy fear as a temptation standing guard at the outset of the journey, giving rise to timidity.

> *Our common experience tells us that it is fear which disturbs us at the beginning of our conversion, fear of that dismaying picture*

> we form for ourselves of the strict life and unwonted austerity
> we are about to embrace. (SS 33.11.6, trans. Walsh, 1976: 154)

AWARENESS OF LOVE

We have seen that the turning of the will begins the conversion experience, a process helped along by humility, self-knowledge, awareness of the sinful state, feeling shame, mourning sin, and turning away from sin through a proper fear of the Lord. But finally, the drawing power of the love of God insists on a response, for such love is God's nature and the root of conversion. Sommerfeldt describes this process as an educated love, one which leads to freedom and happiness: 'Under the impulse of God's grace, the lover grows in imitation of Christ's love. That love, Bernard teaches, will make one free. And that freedom will lead to happiness' (1991: 120).

Bernard directs the soul to Christ the divine educator: 'Christian, learn from Christ how you ought to love Christ. Learn a love that is tender, wise, and strong' (SS 20.3.4, trans. Walsh, 1971, 1: 149).

Bernard writes to Thomas who, having promised himself to Clairvaux, is dithering. Bernard writes to him of love. Unfortunately, the Provost of Beverley dies unexpectedly, his promise still not realised (James, 1998: 158).

> Let no one who loves God have any doubt that God loves him. The love of God for us precedes our love for him and it also follows it. How could he be reluctant to love us in return for our love when he loved us even when we did not love him? I say he loved us. As a pledge of his love you have the Spirit, and you have a faithful witness to it in Jesus, Jesus crucified. A double and irrefutable argument of God's love for us. Christ died and so deserved our love. The holy Spirit works upon us and make us love him. Christ has given us a reason for loving himself, the Spirit the power to love him. (Le 109.8: 162)

IN SEARCH OF FRIENDSHIP

Love's expansion

In a sermon on the Song of Songs, Bernard speaks eloquently of the soul's expansion in love. As love grows, the soul is widened to receive more of the Lord. The soul becomes a roomy place for the Lord to inhabit, with avenues for the Lord to walk. The soul must be directed away from worldly pursuits of lust and power—the entanglement of sin—and grow and expand:

> What a capacity this soul has, how privileged its merits, that it is found worthy not only to receive the divine presence, but to be able to make sufficient room! What can I say of her who can provide avenues spacious enough for the God of majesty to walk in! She certainly cannot afford to be entangled in law-suits nor by worldly cares; she cannot be enslaved by gluttony and sensual pleasures, by the lust of the eyes, the ambition to rule, or by pride in the possession of power. If she is to become heaven, the dwelling-place of God, it is first of all essential that she be empty of all these defects... The soul must grow and expand, that it may be roomy enough for God. Its width is it love... The capacity of any man's soul is judged by the amount of love he possesses; hence he who love much is great, he who loves a little is small, he who has no love is nothing. (SS 27.6.10, trans. Walsh, 1976, 2: 83)

The expansion of love in the soul will be the measure by which a neighbour is loved and this love is not bound to family ties but embraces all in precisely the biblical injunction to love one's neighbour.

> But if his love expands and continues to advance till it outgrows these narrow, servile confines, and finds itself in the open ranges where love is freely given in full liberty of spirit; when from the generous bounty of his goodwill he strives to reach out to all his neighbours, loving each of them as himself, surely one may no longer query, 'What more are you doing than others?' Indeed he has made himself vast. His heart is filled with a love

> that embraces everybody, even those to whom it is not tied by
> the inseparable bonds of family relationship. (SS 27.6.11: 84)

For Bernard, love is neither mushy nor sentimental. It is a force to be reckoned with and should, therefore, be waged as warfare, going towards enemies with openheartedness:

> Progressing further still, you may endeavour to take the kingdom of love by force, until by this holy warfare you succeed in possessing it even to its farthest bounds. Instead of shutting off your affections from your enemies, you will do good to those who hate you, you will pray for those who persecute and slander you, you will strive to be peaceful even with those who hate peace. Then the width, height and beauty of heaven of your soul will be the width, height and beauty of heaven itself. (27.6.1: 84)

BERNARD ON FRIENDSHIP AS FORMATION IN THE LOVE OF GOD

As we have seen, Bernard's life and legacy is fused to the times in which he lived. His period is an age of valiant knights and courtly love where romantic love blossomed and bloomed in all of secular life, spreading to the schools of theology and the universities, encroaching on the monasteries where friendship flourished. As a man steeped in his social environment, Bernard is 'acutely aware of the dynamics of love as a spiritual path' (Cousins, 8: 1987). At the time the sexual relationship between the theologian teacher Peter Abelard and his talented pupil Heloise (c.1101–1163) was a scandal; today it is the stuff of novel and film.

Constant Mews, a medieval historian whose published works are concentrated on Abelard, has analysed the stormy relationship between Bernard and Abelard in great detail (2011: 133–168). Our concern is not with the intricate historical and theological minutiae of the debate, but to use the controversy as a stepping-stone to launch a discussion in general terms into the idea of spiritual friendship as formation at that time. From this examination the particular challenges extracted will point up similarities and differences between the two opponents. These comments will serve as a litmus test for the limits and expansion of friendship in the texts presented for analysis in Bernard's works. It must be stated that Bernard's 'interference' in Abelard's progress as a theologian (as discussed in Chapter 3), is a late entry and long after the events described below— the brutal punishment inflicted on him something in which he was not personally involved.

Abelard and Heloise

In an age of upheaval, philosophers and thinkers are liberated from unchanging formulas and attitudes of orthodox church belief (Schipperges, 1998: 15). First into the ring to throw down the gauntlet is the controversial Abelard, master of the didactic method, offering critical, dialectical and unspiritual teaching in the schools (Knowles, 1962: 87). However, if too easily treated as a dialectician and not marking his spiritual discourse with Heloise, overlooked as a lover with a message (cf. Gilson, 1968: xviii). Heloise is a very brilliant 20-year-old pupil of Abelard, an outstanding education from nuns in letters and languages placing her in a different league from most women of her generation, but with a low opinion of her writing (Flanagan, 1989: 48, 49). The carnality in their relationship is almost over-emphasised by Abelard in a retrospectively written piece, its very physicality drawing attention to the punishment he suffered by an appalling act of castration for his crime. The consolation of the Holy Spirit in taking him into the religious life a contrast to the 'false enthusiasm' of the act of love (Mews, 2011: 144).

> *What more? We were united first in a house, then in spirit. Under the pretext of discipline, we gave ourselves completely to love; study of reading offered the hidden places that love chose, and then with our books open before us, more words of love than of reading passed between us, more kissing than teaching.* (Abelard, Historia Calamitatum (1978) Paris: 72–73, trans. Mews: 143)

FRIENDSHIP IN THE CIRCLE OF ETERNAL LOVE

In their ongoing, copious correspondence by letter and poem, Abelard advocates love which passes from an inferior carnality to a superior, respectful, measured distance. Heloise disagrees: her love has always been pure and they should develop a new intimacy, each from their religious houses, and keep writing to one another. The thinking behind their unique plane of attachment—for the idealistic Heloise a selfless love not yet attained—is made slightly more complex by Abelard's use of a notion from Cicero's pagan text, which was discussed in Chapter 2 (Mews: 144). *De amicitia* (*On Friendship*) has the Platonic idea of a common soul shared only by two very intimate friends, a philosophical symbol Christianised by Abelard and enlarged to encompass not only close friends but the Holy Spirit as a world-soul, the divine goodness (*bonitas*) sustaining creation (Dronke, 1974: 56–57, 82). The convent founded by Abelard for Heloise (1122–1127) and dedicated to the Paraclete (the consoling Holy Spirit) appears to sanctify the search for an exclusive spiritual bonding of love for the few (cf. Flanagan, 1989: 55). After only a few years this innovative community ceased, split by internal division and incapable of holding in unity without a conventional monastic Rule (cf. Mews: 144, 148).

The problematic of a spiritual union based on pagan philosophical ideas is the undoing of Abelard. The first issue is that in orthodox theology the work of the Holy Spirit is specific to the bond between Father and Son and, therefore the Spirit is the go-between, linking the Trinity and human creatures, as discussed in Chapter 2. To subtract divinity and dynamic trinitarian relationship from the Spirit in favour of a cosmic power totally belittles the operations of the Holy Spirit as Person: any spiritual sense or intuition, including intimate friendship, could be said to have its origin in the Paraclete. Clearly, this cannot be the case. However much in love and in a spiritual bond two lovers find their being, does not automatically make that bond a Christian one.

The second issue is in the tussle in Abelard to make sense of love: the distinction between 'desiring-love' (*cupiditas, concupiscentia*) which seeks a reward, and pure love (*caritas, amicitia*), or 'friendship-love', which seeks only the good of the other (Carmichael: 2004, 102–103, and n.8).

The two areas of contention in Abelard viz. the operation of the Holy Spirit and Platonic friendship, can be seen in their differences in light of Bernardine orthodoxy. Cistercian friendship has its origin in unity achieved through the Holy Spirit, the Third Person in the Trinity who is *concordia*, the bond of love. If desire for God is everything, with *affectus* at its heart, then pure friendship with that same desirous intent embarks on a common journey together, never exclusive, toward God. The texts below seek to illustrate, in general terms, these specifics.

THE WAY OF CISTERCIAN FRIENDSHIP AS FORMATION

Far from being prudish about lovers and love, Sommerfeldt observes that, for Bernard, lovers are those who understand and know reality, and the only reality is love: 'The truly happy person is a lover' (1991: 97). In Bernard's life and thoughts on friendship, Sommerfeldt finds a quintessential relationship between spiritual growth and the love between friends: 'The path to perfection is graced by a particularly intense form of love of another. And that is friendship. Friendship is the perfection of the human, and therefore good, need to give and receive intimate affection' (1991: 107).

The way of strengthening the waverer

In Bernard's community there can be no exclusivity and in humility all are called to discern another's truth by learning to understand, to stand in their shoes, to weep or laugh with them. Empathy is a good part of the path to helping others become like Jesus.

> The merciful are quick to see the truth in their neighbours when they feel for them, and unite themselves with them in love so closely that they feel their goods and ills as their own. When the weak suffer, they suffer... with hearts purified by this brotherly love... Those who do not share the troubles of others but, on the contrary, spurn those who weep or mock

> those who are happy, and do not feel in themselves the feelings
> of others because they are not moved by their emotion, how
> can they find the truth in their neighbours? (HUM 3.6: 106)

It is not sufficient to feel with another; you must know yourself and your own mood, and draw on your experience to help your neighbour:

> But to have a heart which is sad because of someone else's
> wretchedness you must first recognise your neighbour's
> mind in your own and understand from your own
> experience how you can help him. (HUM 3.6: 106)

Bernard's exemplar is never another human being, but always Jesus who, in his human nature, 'learned mercy' by submitting himself to human misery and experience. Jesus is the merciful High Priest tested in every way as we are, yet without sin (HUM 3.9: 108–109, Heb. 4:15). In the same way the brothers are to know themselves in their weakness and strengthen the wavering without anger or indignation which destroys. He tells them to

> be aware of what you are, that you are truly wretched, and
> so learn to be merciful, for you can learn it in no other way.
> If you see your neighbour's failing and not your own you will
> be moved not to mercy but to indignation, not to help him
> but to judge him, not instruct him in a spirit of gentleness
> but to destroy him in a spirit of anger. (4.13: 111)

For new disciples wavering in the faith, Bernard waxes lyrical from the Song of Songs about the tender, yet strengthening response of the Bride, that is, the Church (SS 10.1.1–2.3, trans. Walsh, 1971, 1: 61–63). His graphic analogy, which some might find offensive, is to the breasts of the Bride which will bring forth 'the milk of encouragement, compassion, that of consolation', and as often as this 'spiritual mother' receives the kiss of Christ she will feel these virtues flowing from heaven into her heart. From these full breasts of 'consolation' and 'encouragement' will come motherly comfort:

> *For example, if she should notice that one of those whom she begot by preaching the Good News is assailed by temptation, that he becomes emotionally disturbed, is reduced to sadness and pusillanimity and therefore no longer capable of enduring the force of the temptation, will she not condole with him, caress him, weep with him, comfort him, and bring forward every possible evidence of God's love in order to raise him from his desolate state. (2.2: 62)*

The new eager-to-please converts, the Bride will cheer on as a mother, the successful as much as the failing:

> *If, on the contrary, she discovers that he is eager, active, progressive, her joy abounds, she plies him with encouraging advice, fans the fire of his zeal, imparts the ways of perseverance, and inspires him to ever higher ideals. She becomes all things to all, mirrors in herself the emotions of all and so shows herself to be a mother to those who fail no less than to those who succeed. (SS 10.2.2, trans. Walsh, 1971, 1: 62)*

The monastic community listening to these instructions will be in full receipt of Benedict's Prologue to the Rule, understanding that their abbot is endorsing (and embroidering) its sensibilities. Their 'school for the Lord's service' must 'demand nothing that is harsh, nothing oppressive' but, that a 'balance' is brought to bear, there are 'some slight restrictions aimed at the correction of errors and the preservation of love' (RB: 9).

The way of directing the soul

Having outlined practical pastoral care for one another, Bernard does not hold back but ploughs on relentlessly, continuing in Sermon 10 of the Song of Songs to upbraid those whose business it is to direct souls (2.3: 62). These people, presumably clergy, are in it as a business and do not conduct themselves in the way he has just outlined. Bernard is probably referring to the wicked custom of indulgences, whereby a soul's salvation is procured by money deposited into church coffers. Such a procedure precludes any personal interest or involvement in the supplicant to be shown by the professional priest. This is an ecclesiastical legal transaction without spiritual nous or biblical precedent. His protest is against this abhorrence for the 'love of money', which exhibits 'an insatiable passion for gains' and finds rest only when it is free from 'the anxiety of securing, or even further increasing' its acquisitions. The sermon picks up on the deficiencies of such spiritual directors who are 'devoid of the maternal instinct' and are 'fat, gross, bloated' (3.3: 63). True mothers have fatness too, but their breasts are full 'pressing the milk of encouragement' and the 'milk of consolation from the breast of compassion.' With that final remark, Bernard coyly (and sensibly) ends: 'And with that I think we may desist from further discussion on the breasts of the bride and the milk that fills them' (3.3: 63). One can only assume that such was the educated ear of the monks (the use of allegory being commonplace in sermonising) that their thoughts throughout this narrative, and indeed in other suggestive passages from the Song of Songs, remained celestially focussed!

This slight dabbling in Sermon 10 in the feminine imagery customary in Bernard goes a long way toward a possible explanation for his ability to communicate with women, although his language in letters to those of the female gender are never in the mode of the Song of Songs and always remarkably circumspect. However, we find in his letter to the nun Ermengarde formerly Countess (see Chapter 1), exactly those attributes of compassion and consolation expounded in the sermon. An extract from his letter to her will give some idea of how he sees himself—a faithful spiritual counsellor concerned for the welfare of her soul. He is exceedingly pleased to hear of her progress as a nun, having relinquished her former life, and urges her to stick at her new vocation, one which seems to have been encouraged by Bernard:

IN SEARCH OF FRIENDSHIP

> *I have received what has given delight to my heart, the news of your peace. I am glad because you are glad. Your evident joyfulness is a great refreshment to my mind. It has nothing about it of flesh and blood, for now you are living humbly instead of in state, as one of no consequence instead of as a great lady, as poor instead of rich, and you are deprived of the consolation of your brother, son, and home. So without doubt your joyfulness can only be of the Holy Spirit. After having long since conceived of the fear of God you have at last given birth to the spirit of salvation, and love has cast out fear. (Le 120: 182)*

We see Bernard with his spiritual counsellor hat on in the case of his dear friend, William of Saint Thierry, who longs to join the order at Clairvaux. Bernard is against this move, as he sees the importance of William's role in monastic reform by remaining where he is as abbot of his Benedictine house. He works hard at defusing the intensity of their friendship so as not to cloud his judgement and to be in an objective position to discern the way ahead.

> *But putting aside what both of us wish, as it is right we should, it is safer for me and more advantageous for you if I advise you as I think God wishes. Therefore I say hold on to what you have got, remain where you are, and try to benefit those over whom you rule. Do not try to escape the responsibility of your office while you are still able to discharge it for the benefit of your subjects. Woe to you if you rule them and do not benefit them, but far greater woe to you if you refuse to benefit them because you shirk the burden of ruling them (Le 88: 127–28).*

Bernard offers tough love and is unbending on his stance that William's first responsibility is the oversight given the monks in his care. Here is an echo of his insightful advice to Eugenius (see Chapter 3). Both circumstances illustrate Bernard speaking to power, as both equal and subordinate to, and of finding the wherewithal to direct his friends. As a first-rate 'coach' he is not intimidated by the protests of his friend, William, or the status of Eugenius. His first call is to the health of the Church in its broadest sense and that means putting personal likes and dislikes to one side for the sake of true spiritual formation in his friends.

Aelred of Rievaulx has a light touch when it comes to directing the soul of a friend, the accent being on spiritual responsibility for the other. As in Bernard's friendships, this widens the field, cultivating growth and not only pleasure in a friend who is called

> the guardian of love, or, as some prefer, the guardian of the soul itself. Why? Because it is proper for my friend to be the guardian of mutual love or of my very soul, that he may in loyal silence protect all the secrets of my spirit and may bear and endure according to his ability anything wicked he sees in my soul. For the friend will rejoice with my soul rejoicing, grieve with it grieving, and feel that everything that belongs to a friend belongs to himself. (SF 1.20: 59)

The skill of listening in coaching practice tries to encourage space for expression of feelings and thoughts without interruption or interrogation. Aelred recognises that, even within a monastic setting, being heard can be problematic for a quiet person. He addresses his observations of this feature of community life to an anonymous person, but clearly anyone familiar with the feeling of shyness or disengagement in conversation can identify with the feelings expressed:

> Not long ago while I was relaxing among a crowd of brothers, on every side everyone was adding to the din. One was questioning and another debating. One was raising questions about Scripture, another about ethics, a third about the vices, and a fourth about the virtues. You alone were silent. Suddenly raising your head in the group, as you were about to add some remark, your voice seemed to stick in your throat. Then lowering your head, you fell silent. Withdrawing a short distance from us but again returning, you looked crestfallen. From all this I was led

to conclude that, hating crowds and preferring privacy, you
hesitated to express what was on your mind.' (SF 1.2: 55)

The solution to the issue of the very private person is, as Aelred points out through the mouth of the monk Ivo, the desire for a secluded conversation with his abbot 'alone just once, with no others present' in which he may 'lay bare without interruption the ardour of [my] heart' (SF 1.3: 56). Aelred replies with delight, expounding on the benefit of spiritual wisdom coming from a friend:

> I will gladly comply... Speak then without anxiety. Share
> with a friend all your thoughts and cares, that you may
> have something either to learn or to teach, to give and
> to receive, to pour out and to drink in. (SF 1.4: 56)

BERNARD ON FORMATION WITHIN THE FELLOWSHIP OF DIVINE LOVE

Formation in the Cistercian way is a complete lived experience based on the meditation and reading of the Gospel. The practices and exercises of the Order are defended in the *Mirror of Charity*:

> To summarise many things in a few words, I hear nothing about
> perfection in the precepts of either the Gospel or the apostles,
> I find nothing in the writings of the holy Fathers, I understand
> nothing in the sayings of the ancient monks which is not in
> harmony with this order and this profession. (MC 2.17.43: 195)

From a vantage point of the spiritual disciplines, the human condition, overcome by restless anxiety, finds its rest nestled into the crucified Jesus:

> Meanwhile let my soul grow wings, Lord Jesus; I ask, let my soul
> grow wings in the nest of your discipline. Let it rest in the clefts
> of the rock, in the hollow of the wall. [Songs 2:14]. Let my soul

*meanwhile embrace you crucified and take a draught of your
precious blood. Let this sweet meditation meanwhile fill my
memory, lest forgetfulness wholly darken it.* (MC 1.4.16: 95–96)

RESTING IN THE CLEFTS OF THE ROCK

The discipline of dwelling in the cleft of the rock in the shadow of the Almighty is the theme of Bernard's Lenten sermons on Psalm 91. The heading of the series of seventeen sermons is 'He who dwells', the commentary on the psalm a set of spoken exhortations to monks during the specific liturgical season of Lent. Bernard begins his exposition on the journey to the heavenly city in the footstep of Jesus Christ with words about hope, a differentiation which separates those who live in the refuge of the Almighty from those who do not, people without a proper godly hope:

> *The best means of recognising someone who dwells in divine shelter is by looking at those who do not dwell there. You will find they are of three types: the first do not hope; the second have given up hoping; and the third hope in vain. For if anyone fails to make God his refuge, trusting in his own strength and the abundance of his riches, he does not dwell in the shelter of God.* (LS 1.1, trans. Saïd, 1981: 119)

The problem with the first set of people is that they rely on their own efforts, dwelling in the merit of their labours; the second group are full of woe for their weakness and dwell in the frailty of their bodies; the third dwell in lovelessness for God and in the vanity that he will always have mercy on them.

> *The third person's dwelling is unclean, the second's is uneasy, the first's is foolish and reckless... What is more, this dwelling place is crumbling to ruins. What you ought to do is to prop it up and reinforce it rather than live in it.* (LS 1.3:121–22)

Having reinforced the futility of trying to live without hope and in the dwelling of the self, the meditation then proceeds to extol the merits and excellence of the protection afforded people whose shelter is God. They will not wish to lose their dwelling and they seek to maintain their position, which no evil power can undermine.

> The only people who dwell in the shelter of the Most High are those whose sole desire is to receive it, whose sole fear is to lose it, and to ponder it carefully and diligently—which surely is piety, the worship of God. Happy indeed is he who dwells in the shelter of the Most High, for he will abide under the protection of the God of heaven. Is there under heaven anything that could harm the person whom the God of heaven has decided to protect and preserve? The powers of the air are under heaven, this present evil age is under heaven and also the spirit lusting against the flesh. (LS 1.3: 122–23)

Confession

The secret of continual living in the shelter of the Most High is a dedicated effort whereby one returns to the secret places of one's being with a repentant, confessing attitude:

> It now remains for him to link up with the royal road and go forward to truth, and join confession of the lips to contrition of heart, as I have so often urged you to do. 'For man believes with his heart and so is justified, and he confesses with his lips and so is saved.' Turned back to his heart, he must become little in his own eyes, as Truth himself has said, 'Unless you turn back and become like little children, you will never enter the kingdom of heaven.' May he not choose to hide what he knows only too well, that he is reduced to nothing. May he not be ashamed to bring into the light of truth what he cannot see in secret without being moved to pity. In this way man enters the ways of mercy and truth, the ways of the Lord, the ways of life. (LS 11.9: 209–10)

The theme of repentance and turning to Christ is one which runs throughout the Bernadine corpus and must be seen in its context.

Bernard was the 'ambassador of Jesus Crucified, the Saviour of the world. It is not astonishing then that, himself entirely aflame with the love of God, his greatest desire was to save souls, to urge them to conversion, and to win them over to Christ in the monastic life' (Saïd, 1981: 11). Between Lent 1139 and early 1140 Bernard had a stopover in Paris at which he was prevailed upon to address the clergy, to preach the word of God to them. The sermon *On Conversion* is the text of that delivery. In the traditional sense of the word, 'conversion' meant 'becoming a monk', a renunciation of the world (Saïd, 1981: 13). It was a radical decision to enter the cloister, to deny the flesh in taking a vow of celibacy and to surrender to a rule. Monastification is not as familiar to contemporary Christians as it was in the Middle Ages, where abbeys and convents were integral to the economy, education, and church. At that time a choice for Christ in this way set apart a nobleman, a knight, a merchant, a teacher, and the monasteries often became centres of learning, business, music, and culture which influenced for good, as salt and light in society.

Today the Christian does not normally devote herself to a life of removal from the world— the trend of active involvement being the opposite of seclusion: an open door to the world rather than a convent wall. However, there is something we may learn from a principle of starting somewhere, of an initial turning to Christ in a purposeful act of dedication. More to the point for our study is the intriguing notion, somewhat passé it feels in contemporary Christian culture, that turning to Christ in contrition and repentance is not only a one-off drama but part of everyday spiritual formation into the image of God. The ear is tuned to the voice of the Lord, as Bernard cajoles the listening clergy in Paris in his sermon *On Conversion*:

> *May I suggest then that you prick up the ears of your heart in order to hear this inner voice and that you make an effort to hear God speaking within rather than the man speaking without... his voice... pierces all secret things and drives away the sluggishness of souls.* (Cver 1.1.2, trans. Saïd, 1981: 33)

IN SEARCH OF FRIENDSHIP

Speaking to clergy to provoke them to a greater allegiance to Christ is not to be sneered at, even though we might feel that as 'professionals' they are already in service. For Bernard there is always more, his own life a pattern for countless others of sold-out devotion to Jesus Christ and the reason the Church canonised him as a saint. Bernard does not let the mature Christians off the hook. He persistently presses his case to awaken and turn us all to face God and to hear with contrition the insistent voice:

> *Nor do we have much difficulty in hearing this voice; the difficulty is rather in stopping our ears from hearing it. For that voice offers itself, presents itself, and never ceases to knock at the door of each one of us.* (Cver 1.2.3: 33)

The voice of God is also a beam of light, an exposé of darkness in the human soul:

> *For this voice is not only a mighty voice, but it is also a beam of light, both informing men of their transgressions and bringing to light things hidden in darkness. Nor is there any difference between this inward voice and this light, as the one same Son of God is both the Word of the Father and the brightness of his glory... to bring the soul to self-knowledge... It opens the book of the conscience.* (Cver 1.2.3: 34)

The work of the Father and Son in converting the soul is clear from this passage. The voice and the light to reveal sin, and then the fire of the Spirit to purge. Bernard articulates the orthodox Christian assertion that the conviction of the Holy Spirit brings about repentance in the soul (John 16:8). The Spirit, as it were, turns up the heat:

> *Will anyone who comes shivering to a fire and is warmed [by it] question that the heat, which he could not have had without the fire, came to him from it? In the same way, if someone once*

freezing because of his iniquity is afterwards inflamed by a certain fervour of repentance, should he question whether it was another Spirit that had come to him, one who accuses and judges his own? (SSS Pentecost 1.3, trans. Kienzle, 1991: 71)

Formation in the way of Bernard is abandoning friendship with the world and choosing to enlist as a soldier or knight in Christ's armour—a decisive and lifelong commitment lived in the shelter of the Most High God.

GROWING WINGS IN THE NEST OF DISCIPLINE

To grow wings within the nest of monastic discipline is to strengthen and expand spiritually and to attain the heights of contemplation and prayer. It is not a metaphor for taking flight in the natural and escaping the monastery, as Bernard is at pains to point out to his nephew Robert. He is quite put out that this family member has left the Cistercians and selected the abbey of Cluny above his own. He contrasts the easier Cluniac lifestyle of endless liturgy and psalmody with the rigours of Clairvaux: the daily grind of work and sleep, fasting and vigils, manual labour, and silence. Who would want this? Yet, argues Bernard, the principles are scriptural. Hard work and abstemious eating are good for the body and the soul:

Arouse yourself, gird your loins, put aside idleness, grasp the nettle, and do some hard work. If you act thus you will soon find that you only need to eat what will satisfy your hunger, not what will make your mouth water. Hard exercise will restore the flavour to food that idleness has taken away. Much that you would refuse to eat when you had nothing to do, you will be glad of after hard work. Idleness makes one dainty, hard work makes one hungry. It is wonderful how work can make food taste sweet which idleness finds insipid. (Le 1.12: 8)

Ascetic exercises as defined by fasts and prayer vigils must be moderated, as must sleep and psalmody. Bernard is not advocating for his monks a strenuous rule unobtainable and nonsensical but he is asking this family member to see the discipline as lightweight in the light of eternity:

> You have become unaccustomed to our clothes and now you dread them as too cold in winter and too hot in summer… You fear our vigils, fasts, and manual labour, but they seem nothing to anyone who considers the flames of hell. The thought of the outer darkness will soon reconcile anyone to wild solitudes. Silence does not displease when it is considered how we shall have to give an account of every idle word… If we spend well all the night enjoined by the rule in Psalmody, it will be a hard bed on which we cannot sleep. If we labour with our hands as much during the day as we are professed to do, rough indeed will be the fare we cannot eat. (1.12: 8)

Silence

Of the monastic enclosure of Clairvaux, the *Vita prima* imprints in the record the first impressions of William of Saint Thierry: the great silence, a 'midnight hush' which greeted a visitor to that sacred valley:

> In that very hive of activity, where none might be idle but each was busy at his appointed task, a midnight hush would greet the noontide visitor, broken only by work noises or the chanting of the office, as might be. This much-talked-of silence inspired such awe in laymen coming to the monastery that they were afraid to pass any remark that was not essential to their business, let alone a frivolous or improper one… the solitude of that valley, strangled and overshadowed by its thick thickly wooded hills, in which God's servants lived their hidden lives… a crowd of solitaries… the rule of silence, in an ordered crowd of men the order safeguards the solitude of each man's heart. (VP 1.7.35: 31)

William's description conjures up a wonderfully idyllic scene of absolute tranquility in the midst of work, governed by the rule of silence, in which each monk was alone and yet also together in a 'crowd of solitaries.' Well-known lines from a hymn 'Dear Lord and Father of Mankind' composed by a Quaker, John Greenleaf Whittier (1872) echo this love of silence fundamental to the Society of Friends, capturing its eternal essence: the kind of silence so beloved by the Cistercians.

> O Sabbath rest by Galilee,
> O calm of hills above,
> Where Jesus knelt to share with Thee
> The silence of eternity,
> Interpreted by love!

The benefit of silence is to be realised especially in the art of solitary prayer.

Prayer
Praying, whether it be the scriptural texts read prayerfully and meditatively, or the intimate space in which to be with the Lord in prayer and thoughtfulness, prayer is an exercise demanding freedom from distraction. For this, Bernard *commands* solitude. It is, after all, central to the Rule: 'Monks should be silent at all times but especially at night' (RB 42: 65). In a sermon on the Song of Songs he speaks to his soul to be faithful to his Love, even to keep a distance from friends in order to nurture his prayer and to be before the face of Christ. Bernard is advocating a mental, spiritual distance, a kind of boundary setting within the soul, a detachment from outward excitements. At times a physical separation is necessary, particularly for personal prayer:

> O holy soul, remain alone, so that you might keep yourself and
> him alone who you have chosen for yourself out of all that exist.
> Avoid going abroad, avoid even the members of your household;
> withdraw from friends and those you love, not excepting the
> man who provides for your needs. Can you not see how shy your

> Love is, that he will never come to you when others are present?
> Therefore you must withdraw, mentally rather than physically,
> in your intention, in your devotion, in your spirit. For Christ
> the Lord is a spirit before your face, and he demands solitude of
> the spirit more than of the body, although physical withdrawal
> can be of benefit when the opportunity offers, especially in
> time of prayer. (SS 40.3.4, trans. Walsh, 1976, 2: 202)

Jesus is the role model for the monks, hiding from crowds, family and friends and spending nights alone in prayer. But solitude is so much more than an action done at a certain time or place. It is so easy to take to oneself the matters and affairs of everyone else, of the 'masses' (how easy in a world of instant social media). To retain an inner posture of solitariness requires the cultivation of a habit of withdrawal from worldly matters such as gossip, arguments, wrong-doing:

> You enjoy this solitude if you refuse to share in the common gossip,
> if you shun involvement in the problems of the hour and set no
> store by the fancies that attract the masses; if you reject what
> everybody covets, avoid disputes, make light of losses, and pay no
> heed to injuries. Otherwise you are not alone even when alone. Do
> you not see that you can be alone when in company and in company
> when alone? However great the crowds that surround you, you
> can enjoy the benefits of solitude if you refrain from curiosity
> about other people's conduct and shun rush judgement. Even if
> you should see your neighbour doing what is wrong, refuse to pass
> judgement on him, excuse him instead. (SS 40.3.5: 202–203)

The heart of prayer is love for Jesus the God-man, and Bernard speaks eloquently of the relationship to be desired above all else, advising especially the beginner on the path of love to employ some kind of image of the incarnation. Today we might consider using a holding cross, or a palm cross. The main point of the prayer is that we are attracted to Christ in his earthly body, that our carnal natures identify with his humanity, making Jesus more accessible to us. However, Bernard wishes this carnal human nature, at first drawn to the love of the very human Jesus, to be elevated to a greater, spiritual love:

> *The soul at prayer should have before it a sacred image of the God-man, in his birth or infancy or as he was teaching, or dying, or rising, or ascending. Whatever form it takes this image must bind the soul with the love of virtue and expel carnal vices, eliminate temptations and quiet desires. I think this is the principal reason why the invisible God willed to be seen in the flesh and to converse with men as a man. He wanted to recapture the affections of carnal men who were unable to love in any way, by first drawing them to the salutary love of his own humanity, and then gradually to raise them to a spiritual love.* (SS 20.5.6, trans. Walsh, 1971, 1: 152)

For Bernard, prayer is a discipline, a studied intent developed into a habit. For this reason, he speaks to his brother monks about vigilance, about paying attention to the movements of their souls in order to purify their hearts and cling to God steadfastly and in the manner of the psalmist David. They will be rewarded by visions of angels. What an incentive to prayer for hard-working monks in the granges, choirs, and liturgies of the monastic routine:

> *This adherence to God is nothing less than that vision of God granted as a unique favour only to the pure in heart. That David had this clean heart is evident from his words: "My soul clings close to you" [Psa.63:8]; and again: "My joy lies in being close to God" [Psa. 73:28]. His vision of God brought him close to God, his closeness assured the vision. The man who lives in this state habitually will have the angels for his frequent and familiar guests, especially if they frequently find him in prayer.* (SS 7.7, trans. Walsh, 1971, 1: 43)

The habit of prayer is a duty and a responsibility. The sensible affections are not the goal of prayer and Bernard is quite indifferent to how a monk might *feel* when at prayer. Nevertheless, he is far from insensitive to the affections (as we have seen) and he relishes the thought that prayer can be emotional at times. In a period of intense spiritual drought, there can arise an unexpected infusion of grace to flood the soul with love and fervour for God:

> Men with an urge to frequent prayer will have experience of what I say. Often enough when we approach the altar to pray our hearts are dry and lukewarm. But if we persevere, there comes an unexpected infusion of grace, our breast expands as it were, and our interior is filled with an overflowing love; and if somebody should press upon it then, this milk of sweet fecundity would gush forth in streaming richness. (SS 9.5.7, trans. Walsh, 1971, 1: 58)

Prayer is not only personal, but corporate worship is incumbent upon every monk as set down in the Rule for the daily offices. This is the rigorous strength of worship and Bernard is concerned to emphasise that not even ruminating out loud upon the scriptural text must detract from that duty. It is a call to arms, to man up and speak up:

> I exhort you to participate always in the divine praises correctly and vigorously, that you may stand before God with as much zest as reverence, not sluggish, not drowsy, not yawning, not sparing your voices, not leaving words half-said or skipping them, not wheezing through the nose with an effeminate stammering, in a weak and broken tone, but pronouncing the words of the Holy Spirit with becoming manliness and resonance and affection; and correctly, that while you chant you ponder on nothing but what you chant. (SS 47.3.8, trans. Walsh and Edmonds, 1979, 3: 9–10)

FILLING THE MEMORY WITH SWEET MEDITATION

Bernard does not espouse modern methods of mindfulness or mental prayer—meditation and prayer are more-or-less the same;

FRIENDSHIP IN THE CIRCLE OF ETERNAL LOVE

and meditation, contemplation, and reading are more-or-less the same. Pondering Scripture is, however, the starting point for many matters concerning meditation, for example, the world around, human nature, or the nature of God. The discipline of reading can be strenuous and Bernard labours the point that the receiving of revelatory truth to impart to others is no mean feat for the labouring teacher. Clearly Bernard speaks of himself when he explains to the brothers that

> *no small effort and fatigue are involved in going out day by day to draw waters from the open streams of the Scriptures and provide for the needs of each of you, so that without exerting yourselves you may have at hand spiritual waters for every occasion, for washing, for drinking, for cooking of foods. God's word is a water of the wisdom that saves; when you drink it you are made clean.* (SS 22.1.2, trans. Walsh, 1976, 2: 15)

The monastic practice of a meditative reading upon Scripture is demonstrated in the extremely slow pace of the sermons, or running commentary on the *Song of Songs*. The 86 *Sermons*, composed over 18 years cover only chapters 1 and 2 to chapter 3, verse 1. The Vulgate (the Latin text) is Bernard's source and is only 91 lines of text (Sommerfeldt, 1991: 79, n.53). Deep reading, in-depth dwelling in the words is the stuff of the practice of *lectio Divina* the divine reading of Scripture. One begins with the text, with the life of Christ, and proceeds to other matters. The *lectio*, the prayerful reading of Scripture, is the lynchpin for the spiritual life. We find that Bernard is steeped in the Benedictine tradition and the daily reading of its Rule which pinpoints the *lectio* as that cornerstone (Sommerfeldt, 1991: 75–77).

Scripture

In Sermon 7 on the Song of Songs, Bernard upbraids the monks for dozing off in the psalm singing during the night office. He fully expects them to be attentive, at the ready, ruminating on the truths before them:

> [I]t makes me sad to see some of you deep in the throes of sleep during the night office ... like corpses. (SS 7.4.4, trans. Walsh, 1971, 1: 41)

He himself is so in touch with Scripture that he can exhort his community of monks with a menu of delights awaiting the eager devourer of the biblical passages. Such a one voraciously chews the words out loud by singing, simultaneously feasting on the morsels in the mind. These are actions both physical and intellectual, exercises in spiritual mastication described poetically for the monks gathered to hear teaching on the subject:

> As food is sweet to the palate, so does a psalm delight the heart. But the soul that is sincere and wise will not fail to chew the psalm with the teeth as it were of the mind, because if he swallows it in a lump, without proper mastication, the palate will be cheated of the delicious flavour, sweeter even than honey that drips from the comb. [Psa.19:10]. (SS 7.4.4–5, trans. Walsh, 1971, 1: 41–42)

In Sermon 7, having expounded on the delights awaiting the monks at the table of the Lord, Bernard proceeds to an explanation of the role of the companions of the Bridegroom, those in Solomon's train (Song of Songs 3:6). By a process of allegory based on Psalm 68:27 those attending the King become angelic princes of Zebulun and Naphtali, 'whose work is the praise of God, who live lives of continence [self-restraint], lives of contemplation'. These have 'singleness of purpose of contemplatives'. Based on the Vulgate interpretation of Genesis 49:21, Naphtali is a swift deer, a hind 'whose powers of agile leaping signify the ecstatic ardours of the contemplative mind. As the hind penetrates the wood's dark avenues, so does the contemplative spirit penetrate the obscure meaning of things' (7.5.6: 42–43).

Bernard the preacher extracts from the text an allegorical image of a single-minded contemplative living a life of praise to God, bounding like a deer into the deepest darkness, peering intently into things secret and obtuse to find meaning. These difficult and hidden passages of Scripture are uncovered especially when one turns to the Lord and repents of past experiences. The abbot is exerting pressure on his monks to engage with Scripture so as to plumb its depths for a higher meaning hidden therein and made known to a penitent sinner. Sermon 1 of the Song of Songs places a monk's feet firmly on the rock, which is Christ, so that a new song sounds from the lips and the mystery of revelation is made plain for the seeker of God as

> *texts of Scripture hitherto dark and impenetrable at last become bright with meaning for you, then, in gratitude for this nurturing bread of heaven you must charm the ears of God with a voice of exaltation and praise, a festival song.* (SS 1.5.9, trans. Walsh, 1971, 1: 5)

Bernard points to the work of the Spirit in enlightening the mind and bringing forth revelation from the inspired texts: 'Now under the Spirit's guidance, let us try to draw out the spiritual fruit contained in them.' (SS 51.1.2, trans. Walsh and Edmonds, 1979, 3: 40). Or, in a slightly different translation of the same text (Sommerfeldt 1991: 77): 'to extract the meaning which lies underneath the rind of the letter', which shows that there is a higher meaning or a prophetical sense (the fruit) beneath the 'rind' (the literal words on the page).

Consideration

As we have seen, for Bernard, self-reflection is the bedrock of acquiring self-knowledge and humility. His use of the terms 'meditation' or 'consideration' appear interchangeable. We have applied 'meditation' specifically to Scripture. Here we look at the meaning of 'consideration'. It seems that, for Bernard, reason is used in meditation or consideration but graced with God's inspiration it is not limited to the bounded world of common-sense. The mind or rationality is sanctified by the gift of inspiration, as is the case in a divinely inspired reading of a biblical text:

> *The word of God, winged with the Holy Spirit's fire, can cook the raw reflections of the sensual man, giving them a spiritual meaning that feeds the mind, and inspiring him to say: 'My heart became hot within me, and as I meditated a fire burst forth.'* [Psa. 38:4]. (SS 22.2, trans. Walsh, 1976, 2: 15)

Consideration soars away from the essential and practical, from the rational scientific scrutiny of everything, to enter the realm of speculation, which is indeed the contemplation of God assisted by the Spirit. Using the senses in an orderly, disciplined way, and diligently pondering all things in order to know God, is completely satisfactory and useful. These ways laboriously and quietly lead to God, and the contemplation of God, which is the highest mode of meditation, is the fruit of earnest practical wisdom and study. By meditation or consideration, one is led to the good way, to right relationships lived in just actions towards one another:

> *For the mind must first reflect upon itself to deduce the norm of justice which is not to do to another what one would not wish done to himself, not deny another what one wishes for himself* [Matt. 7:12]. (Csi 1.8.10, trans. Anderson and Kennan, 1976: 39–40)

Bernard understands that love of another person proceeds 'as a result of contemplating such great mercy so undeserved, such generous and proven love' of God. A 'thoughtful mind when it considers them carefully' will not settle for anything less than a godly desire (LG 4.13: 184). From considering and receiving God's love, one can then love another less known:

> *I believe that he who understands this will recognise clearly enough why God is to be loved, that is, why he deserves to be*

loved... And so it is not surprising that a man should love the less someone whom he knows less well (cf. Luke 7:47). (LG 5.14: 185)

Because love comes from God as divine, unmerited favour, is there anything the human being can give in return? Clearly there is. Bernard is at pains to draw out not only the process by which this supernatural love is given, but also to express the notion that our love is the response to God who has given his all, his very life for us. Whimsically, he suggests that even an unbeliever may reason out the sequence of love: that given by God and then returned by a mere mortal. One with the eyes of faith will love more, understanding the love of the cross whereby God proves his love:

> What shall I give to God in return for all these things (Psa. 116:12)? Reason and natural justice press the unbeliever to give himself up wholly to him from whom he has everything, and to love him with all his heart. Faith urges me to love more than that him whom I know to have given me not only myself but his own self. When the age of faith had not yet come God had not made himself known in the flesh, died on the Cross, risen from the tomb, returned to the Father, or proved his great love for us (Rom. 5:8), about which I have said so much; when he had not yet commanded man to love the Lord his God with all his heart, with all his soul, and with all his strength (Deut. 6:5), that is, with all he is, all he knows, all he can do. (LG 4.5: 185)

Bernard's theology of the love of God is simple: first, we are given life as his created creatures; second, he gave up his life for us which gave us back our lives:

> In the first act he gave me myself; in the second he gave me himself; and when he did that he gave me back myself. Given and given again, I owe myself in return for myself, twice over. What am I to give God in return for himself? For even if I could give myself a thousand times over, what am I to God (cf. Job 3:9,14)? (LG 4.5: 186)

IN SEARCH OF FRIENDSHIP

We have come full circle in the gift of love and what better way to end than with the contemplation of God.

Contemplation

It is not always clear what Bernard meant by contemplation. It is a transcendent experience defying explanation. It is a feeling; it is not rational. Contemplation cannot be experienced in the language of reason alone. Contemplation is the experience of a lover (Sommerfeldt 1991: 215–220). Bernard puts it thus:

> This kind of ecstasy, in my opinion, is alone or principally called contemplation. Not to be gripped during life by material desires is a mark of human virtue; but to gaze without the use of bodily likenesses is the sign of angelic purity. Each, however, is a divine gift, each is a going out of oneself, each a transcending of self, but in one goes much farther than in the other. (SS 52.3.5, trans. Walsh, 1979, 3: 53)

For Bernard, the uplifting gaze upon the heavenly city, the bliss of the individual soul or of the Church at repose in the rock which is Christ—the Word of God—is a state of glory. At this moment, the soul or even the Church may be enraptured in ecstasy, raised up by the finger of God. This position in the presence of the Almighty leads to the fear of God (SS 62.3.4 trans. Walsh and Edmonds, 1979, 3: 154–155).

This view of contemplation seems a far cry from the consideration or meditation on the state of one's own soul, and indeed it is. In this case, there is an entirely different discipline. The disciple is concerned with contemplating, searching out and scrutinising the will of God. The searcher must set the gaze mentally upon the witness of the saints and, more importantly, upon Jesus crucified. This is a dutiful action in obedience to the call to purity. To contemplate in such an intentional way is to enter into the healing and transforming power of God. When this occurs, the inner vision is renewed and the

FRIENDSHIP IN THE CIRCLE OF ETERNAL LOVE

seeker may gaze upon the Lord with complete confidence (Bernard, 62.3.4–5, 4.6-7, trans. Walsh and Edmonds, 1979, 3: 154–160).

To close this chapter, we remind ourselves of the circle which represents the love of God. We may begin at any point on that eternal round—forming friendships in the love of God or forming a deeper affection for Jesus or allowing friendship to form the self in the love of God—and we shall be led through a cycle of friendship with others and God. To keep steady and balanced within that diurnal round we develop spiritual habits of reading Scripture, prayer both personal and corporate, seeking solitude and silence, the practical wisdom of consideration and the private act of contemplation of the divine mysteries.

CONCLUSION

We have blazed a trail through an inordinate quantity of unfamiliar material in order to extract from the writings of Bernard of Clairvaux palpable, trustworthy, and workable concepts to invigorate friendship today. We have followed what may be lightly termed a paperchase, tracking down texts to interpret and apply, a strenuous effort on the part of the reader and requiring a great deal of hard work. Now we must find meaning and relevance from this mountain of information in a Cistercian landscape, to place as markers in the topography which is our information-overloaded universe. How may we proceed with such a gargantuan task going forward?

I invite you to consider three crucial features on the twelfth-century map of spirituality, which you might see as roadblocks rather than signs, but which are clear waymakers for contemporary path finders: finances, freedom, formation.

Finances

At no point in our study on love and friendship is payment ever an issue. If the love of money is the root of all evil then monastic life must be extremely pure and good. Money is simply not an object and does not feature, unless as a warning of the distraction of riches and, in the case of simony, payment for sins forgiven—clearly not an option. Why might this be important for a study on love and friendship? We live in an age of professional counselling and therapy, transactional services usually rendered in exchange of monies. Penniless monks lived without recourse to such luxuries. They lived in company with others, confessing their sins, keeping short accounts with God and one another, and generally living happy lives. If the financial burden of contracted professional help could be lifted by a society of praying, accountable Christians, how might that help the debt-ridden others, the downcast and depressed impoverished? And if a shift is made from signing on for years of cash-strapping consultations to receiving mercy and grace from the coffers of Christ in community, how might that create a new dependency upon one another? If, in the first instance there is not an exchange of money for the cure of the soul, but a spiritual habit framing the life that must surely be life-giving and empowering.

This is not to say that therapy and counselling are no-go areas, just as the doctor's surgery is part and parcel of everyday life, but that their place must be seen in relation to all spiritual formation, a business involving the human soul and in which God through Christ Jesus has been at work for 2,000 years. The Church as a caring community has responsibility for its members and cannot simply siphon off people, who stand in need of care, to secular organisations, without first finding the time to listen, to discern, to invite the Holy Spirit and then to wait for God to speak and do his work in prayer. There are gifts or *charisms* which God has placed in local church for just such a purpose and these are gifts of people equipped by the Lord to do the work of ministry and they need to be used.

Freedom

The freedom of a healing relationship in Christ can be life-saving and, as we have seen, a very important part of friendship. To find a point of contact with another whereby one is brought face to face with the self, its fears and anxieties, its joys and blessings, is to live out the truth of the Pauline admonition: 'It is for freedom that Christ set us free. Stand firm, therefore, and refuse to submit again to the yoke of slavery.' (Gal. 5:1). Such freedom has been bought with a price, the precious blood of Jesus Christ and, therefore, should not be relinquished in return for anything inferior. The cross brings reconciliation between estranged people, and the fruits of the atoning work of Jesus stand for every generation and in each and every Christian. Everyone who turns to the Lord may receive this divine favour on their friendships.

Freedom through confession of sins one to another, freedom through the sharing of burdens in prayer, freedom through the knowledge that I am loved by a friend, accepted, prayed for. Freedom in friendship to speak the truth, to hold accountable, to dare to be different from the world and to hold on to friends even when there is upset and pain. To grow together, to laugh and to grieve—this is the legacy for which Christ died. This is often the beginning of true spiritual formation—friends who will not let me go but who hold me through thick and thin—God doing his work in my soul simultaneously. And the challenge of these friends who, through their love for the Lord, incite me to love him more, to pray more, to worship and to praise. When friends stretch me so that I seek Christ and am changed then charity is at work, the pure love which brings total freedom. And healing.

Formation
And finally, formation in, through and by the work of Jesus Christ and in the power of the Holy Spirit. The monastic legacy of handing on the pattern, the order, the rule for others. Paul started this tradition by writing of himself to the church at Thessalonica that he might have made his weight felt but that he was 'as gentle with you as a nurse caring for her children' (1 Thess. 2:7). To the Galatian church he writes: 'You are my own children, and I am in labour with you all over again until you come to have the form of Christ' (Gal. 4:19). These are not only tender terms of endearment but full of the truth of which Jesus spoke, that it is the Spirit that gives life; the flesh is useless (John 6:63). Spiritual formation is a labour of love in and through the Holy Spirit, who uses human beings—a Paul, Bernard, Aelred, Hildegard, Julian of Norwich, or indeed any Tom, Dick or Harriette with that divine grace and gift—to pray, to fast, to intercede, to speak truth, and to love another into the form of Christ.

As we have seen, monastic formation is not a mechanical act of ticking a box of rules, but a relationship with God and the abbot is a key in the application of the rule to the life of the monk. But the monk, too, has a responsibility before God to keep the rule. We do not have such a rule, or at least most Christians are 'saved' by grace from such restrictions. That is the current thinking. However, as we have been at pains to point out, cooperation with God does not come naturally to the flesh and we need the spiritual disciplines of abstemious eating, prayer, worship, scant attention to clothing, Bible reading, worship and silence—a list of which virtues the New Testament is full and which would be tedious to recount, so long would that list be.

A NOTE ON GENRE AND MEDIEVAL TEXTS

SERMON

In its origins the genre of a sermon i.e. the spoken word (*sermo*) connotes spontaneity and development on the spur of the moment and in sync with the reactions of its hearers. This method changed over the course of time and in the wake of classical Greek and Latin writers the medieval composer never wrote without first drawing up an outline or a plan. In medieval monastic literature the sermon (*sermo*) is the most typical literary genre. The sermon could have been the notes of a member of the audience as a skeletal first copy, or the scribblings of a preacher on a tablet of wax, which later was edited and revised by the speaker or a copyist. Bernard would have followed the convention of the time and dictated (*dictare*), meaning composed on wax tablets as a type of rough copy which could be modified and changed. His composition would have been out loud and delivered to his own hand or to the hand of a scribe. After this initial process the writing (*scribere*) would be copyedited by another, or by the composer.

TREATISE

A treatise or tractate (*tractatus*) had a preconceived structure and was a formal and systematic written discussion of a subject.

LIFE

A Life (*Vita*) was a written account or study of a saint, in vogue from the early Church to the end of the Middle Ages. The word 'hagiography' is used to denote the genre. It derives from the Greek words *hagios* meaning 'holy' or 'saint' and *grapho* meaning 'to write'. Hagiography is a written discussion of the life of the saint but it is not strictly biographical. A Life would attempt to capture the essence of the saint's works, teachings and miracles, but inevitably relied on embellishment of virtues, signs and wonders to exaggerate the sanctity of life and to speed up canonisation i.e. the making of a saint by the Church.

LETTER

The standard form of the letter (*epistola*) in monastic medieval literature adhered to the careful and correct style of letter-writing at that time: the salutation, securing of good will, narration, petition, and conclusion. This formula was broken up by a seasoned communicator like Bernard for variation and impact on the reader. A letter served as conversation or a sermon and was saturated in scriptural text. Letters were read out loud by the individual recipient or by an appointed person to the assembly. Monastic mail could be advisory, encouragement in trials, inspirational, consoling; matters of business, friendship, and doctrine. As someone in a high position, Bernard would have engaged special messengers to carry his letters which bore his personal seal. As a highly influential personage, Bernard's persuasive letters reached many and his counsel was widely sought. The total number of authentic letters in the Latin editions, extant in almost 400 manuscripts, is 500 (Kienzle, 1998: viii–x, xv).

A NOTE ON THE WORKS OF BERNARD OF CLAIRVAUX

Bernard wrote in Latin and, unless otherwise indicated, words which are italicised in the text of *In Search of Friendship* will usually be in Latin for titles of works, or for theological and poetic terms. Biblical references in citations from Bernard do not correspond to English translations as they are from the Latin Vulgate or the Greek Septuatint (LXX) and differ slightly in chapter or verse.

SERMONS FROM BERNARD'S WORKS USED IN THIS STUDY

On the Song of Songs (Sermo super Cantica canticorum)

These 86 sermons are a series begun in 1135 and left unfinished at his death in 1153. According to the manuscript tradition and the chronological data, it is possible to say that despite a busy travelling schedule, Bernard put into circulation four groupings:

Sermons 1–24 — completed in 1138
Sermons 24–49 — edited and completed in 1145
Sermons 50–83 — completed in 1148
Sermons 84–86 — completed and work in progress at his death in 1153

The sermons are composed in a literary style, that is to say, without speaking before an audience and are marked by Bernard's own editing and revisions. Unlike the shorter and diverse treatises, letters, and sermons *The Sermons on the Song of Songs* are marked by a unity of theme imposed by the topic and biblical text (Leclercq, 1980: x–xii). From early on in Bernard's life as a monk, the biblical text held him captive, its themes never far from his thinking: 'He found matter there for reflection on current affairs, on his own personal experiences, on human life and the love of God. It proved both a book about the present and particular and a hymn to eternal things' (Evans, 1987: 209).

The translations of Sermons 1–86 from the Cistercian Fathers series 4, 7, 31, and 40 are based on the critical Latin edition prepared by Jean Leclercq, C. H. Talbot, and H. M. Rochais under the sponsorship of the Order of Cistercians and published by Editiones Cistercienses, Piazza Tempio di Diana 14, Rome.

On Conversion, a Sermon to Clerics (Sermo ad clericos de conversione)

This work states that it is a sermon, yet in parts it is formatted as a treatise with headings. Bernard's greatest desire is to win souls to Christ and to conversion to the monastic life. The word 'conversion' is employed in the traditional sense and taken to mean 'becoming a monk', although for Bernard it is also conversion of the heart. On his way back from one of his many business trips, probably at a date between Lent 1139 and the early part of 1140, Bernard stopped in Paris and was prevailed upon to address the students and scholars from the schools of Paris, perhaps in the cloister of Notre Dame. A great many gathered to hear the famed Abbot of Clairvaux. The impact of the sermon was the 'conversion', the purposeful declaration for Christ, of 23 people to the monastic life. These followed Bernard to Clairvaux and were lasting professions to the order (Evans, 1987: 65). The process of personal 'monastification' was to embrace the celestial life, the angelic life—in ancient tradition, the renunciation of the body for celibacy (Saïd, 1981: 12-14). For some of these converts, a declaration for Christ was a brand-new and radical allegiance. The clerics, on the other hand, had already offered their lives for God's service in a full-time capacity. Bernard believes that only the monastery walls can offer complete protection and vigilance against the temptations and wiles of sin and the world. However, not all are called to this life and the sermon will sift souls as Bernard, like Simon the fisherman preaches in order to 'let down the net of the word today' which is no less than the voice of the Lord (§1, trans. Saïd, 1981: 32).

This sermon is a translation of *Ad clericos de conversione*; based on the critical edition of Jean Leclercq and H. M. Rochais (1966) *Sancti Bernardi Opera*, vol. 4: 69–116. Rome: Editiones Cistercienses.

Lenten Sermons on the Psalm 'He who dwells' (Sermo super psalmum 'Qui habitat')

The series of 17 sermons on Psalm 90 (Bernard uses the Latin Vulgate translation, English Psalm 91) are exhortations to monks written during the period of Lent c.1139. Whether these sermons were delivered spontaneously or written up in the style of a sermon and never actually spoken to an audience, is a debatable point. What is not under scrutiny is the content: a Christian pilgrimage from conversion to consummation at the gateway of the eternal city, a journey of the soul which follows Christ. The commentary on the psalm is one of the most famous and beautiful of Bernard's writings and is considered to be one of the 'jewels' of medieval Christian literature (Saïd, 1981: 84–85).

This sermon is a translation of *Sermones in quadragesima de psalmo 'Qui habitat'*; based on the critical edition of Jean Leclercq and H. M. Rochais (1966) *Sancti Bernardi Opera*, vol. 4: 383–492. Rome: Editiones Cistercienses.

Pentecost Sermons (Sermo in die sancto Pentecostes)

These sermons form part of the corpus of 120 liturgical sermons revised and redacted in Bernard's later life (1148–1153). The sermons would be preached and written for the Feast Day of Pentecost.

This translation is based on the critical edition of Jean Leclercq, H. M. Rochais and C. H. Talbot (1968) *Sancti Bernardi Opera*, vol. 5: 121–126. Rome: Editiones Cistercienses.

A NOTE ON THE WORKS OF BERNARD OF CLAIRVAUX

TREATISES FROM BERNARD'S WORKS USED IN THIS STUDY

On the Steps of Humility and Pride (De gradibus humilitatis et superbiae)
By 1124 Bernard had set down what was to become the first of his published works, his writing on the doctrine of humility. It was commissioned by Godfrey of Langres, who, as Prior of Clairvaux, had heard the abbot speak on this topic on a number of occasions. Sent to be Abbot of Fontenay, Godfrey requested these talks in a book for use with his own monks. The book treats of the intimate relationship between pride and humility, although it is less about humility and more about pride, a subject about which Bernard writes from first-hand experience.

Translations from Jean Leclercq, H. M. Rochais, and C. H. Talbot (eds) (1957–1980) *Sancti Bernardi Opera*, 8 vols. Rome: Editiones Cistercienses.

On Loving God (De diligendo Deo)
The treatise was written at some point between 1125, when Bernard wrote his letter about loving God to the monks of the Grande Chartreuse, and 1141 and the death of Aimeric, a good friend of Clairvaux and cardinal deacon and chancellor of the Church of Rome, who had asked Bernard to write a book on loving God.

Translations from Jean Leclercq, H. M. Rochais, and C. H. Talbot (eds) (1957–1980) *Sancti Bernardi Opera*, 8 vols. Rome: Editiones Cistercienses.

On Grace and Free Choice (De gratia et libero arbitrio)
The dogmatic basis for Bernard's theological and mystical works lies in this treatise which deals with the essential problem of grace and freedom in the Letter to the Romans. As an early work written about 1128, it must be seen in the light of the choices Bernard was making on the cusp of his entry into public spheres of influence. Urged by his great friend, William of Saint-Thierry, to whom he addresses the script, Bernard sets out his dogma to the monastic theologian, himself an expert on grace and free will (O'Donovan, 1988: 4–5, 14).

This translation is based on the critical Latin edition prepared by Jean Leclercq, C. H. Talbot, and H. M. Rochais under the sponsorship of the Order of Cistercians and published by Editiones Cistercienses, Piazza Tempio di Diana 14, Rome.

Five Books on Consideration: Advice to a Pope (De consideratione)
This treatise is directed at Eugenius III who became pope in 1145. As a Cistercian monk Bernard knows him to be ambivalent and uncertain about his high office. During the next decade Bernard wrote the first book followed by four more, advising Eugenius to pursue his spiritual life in the midst of the daily pressure of papal affairs.

This translation is based on the critical Latin edition prepared by Jean Leclercq, C. H. Talbot, and H. M. Rochais under the sponsorship of the Order of Cistercians and published by Editiones Cistercienses, Piazza Tempio di Diana 14, Rome.

TREATISES FROM OTHER WRITERS USED IN THIS STUDY

Mirror of Charity (Speculum caritatis)
This is a treatise on the excellence and virtue of charity and is a commission given by Bernard of Clairvaux to Aelred of Rievaulx (1110–1167), 'the most powerful Cistercian in England' (Dutton, 2010: 18). Sections of it probably written prior to 1142 then redacted to the present work in the following few years.

This translation is based on the critical edition of C. H. Talbot, *Liber de speculo caritatis*, Turnhout: Corpus Christianorum Continuatio Mediaevalis.

On Spiritual Friendship (De spirituali amicitia)
By means of internal evidence of historical data, this tractate can be dated from some time after 1147 and completed in 1167. The work, a series of conversations among friends in a monastery, is a spiritual treatise on friendship by Aelred of Rievaulx.

The translation of *De spiritali amicitia* by Lawrence Braceland, SJ, is used with permission of The Archives of the Jesuits in Canada.

A NOTE ON THE WORKS OF BERNARD OF CLAIRVAUX

LETTERS FROM BERNARD'S WORKS USED IN THIS STUDY
1, 12, 13, 51, 73, 87, 88, 89, 109, 119, 120, 121, 125, 129, 147, 151, 177, 179, 205, 305, 306, 307, 308, 326, 390, 424

Translations from Jean Leclercq, H. M. Rochais and C. H. Talbot (eds) (1957–1977) *Sancti Bernardi Opera*, 8 vols. Rome: Editiones Cistercienses.

HAGIOGRAPHY FROM BERNARD'S WORKS USED IN THIS STUDY

Life of Malachy (Vita sancti Malachiae)
Bernard wrote this Life—his only work of hagiography—as a tribute of love and friendship after the death in 1148 of Malachy, who was his not only his contemporary and dear friend, but a reforming archbishop who held exactly the same ideals of disdaining possessions and glorying in the preached Gospel.

Translations from Jean Leclercq, H. M. Rochais, and C. H. Talbot (eds) (1957–1977) *Sancti Bernardi Opera*, 8 vols. Rome: Editiones Cistercienses.

HAGIOGRAPHY OF BERNARD USED IN THIS STUDY

Life of Bernard (Vita prima Bernardi)
The first book of the *Vita prima*, Bernard's hagiography, was completed by his great friend William of Saint Thierry before his death in 1148. It comprises the reminiscences and memories of a friendship of 30 years, covering the early period of Clairvaux. The second book was taken up after Bernard's death by Arnald, abbot of the Benedictine house of Bonneval and is concerned with Bernard's legacy in the eight-year papal schism. The third, fourth and fifth books were written up by Geoffrey of Auxerre, who followed Bernard quite dramatically out of the Paris schools after his sermon on conversion, settling at Clairvaux as secretary to the abbot. Geoffrey accentuates the healing miracles and the way in which people flocked to see and to hear him on his many journeys.

Translations from Jean Leclercq, H. M. Rochais, and C. H. Talbot (eds) (1957–1977) *Sancti Bernardi Opera*, 8 vols. Rome: Editiones Cistercienses.

CHRONOLOGY OF THE LIFE AND TIMES OF BERNARD OF CLAIRVAUX

1073–1085 Pope Gregory VII attacks corruption, especially simony in the church; insists on clerical celibacy; asserts sole right to appoint bishops; the first medieval reformation; dies in exile in Salerno—Empire and Papacy struggle

1090 Bernard born in Fontaines-lès-Dijon, Burgundy; son of a knight Tescelin and Aleth de Montbard; five brothers and one sister

1096–1099 First Crusade

1098 Beginnings of Cistercian monasticism; Robert establishes the 'New Monastery' which becomes Cîteaux

c.1106 Bernard's mother dies; Bernard schooled by canons in Châtillon-sur-Seine

1108 Stephen Harding elected Abbot of Cîteaux

1110 Aelred of Rievaulx born in Hexham, England

1111–1113 Bernard starts an informal monastic community at Châtillon; recruits brothers and uncles; Bernard's family and friends accepted at Cîteaux

1115 Bernard sent by Stephen to found a daughter Cistercian house at Clairvaux in Champagne; Bernard Abbot of Clairvaux

1118 First daughter house of Clairvaux Trois Fontaines

CHRONOLOGY OF THE LIFE AND TIMES OF BERNARD OF CLAIRVAUX

1118–1153	65 daughter houses established during Bernard's abbacy
1119	Constitution for Cistercian Order *Carta Caritas* (Charter of Charity); Bernard ill outside Clairvaux for a year
1120	William of Saint Thierry Benedictine abbot visits Bernard; first writer of *Vita prima*
1125	Bernard's first work *Apology to William* on art and architecture
1115–1125	Bernard's first published work *On the Steps of Humility and Pride*
1125–1141	Bernard writes the treatise *On Loving God*
1128	Bernard writes the treatise *On Grace and Free Choice*
1130–1138	Papal schism; Bernard travels extensively for this cause; intervenes to support the victorious Innocent II
1135–1153	Bernard composes and delivers 86 sermons on the Song of Songs
1138	Bernard's lament for his brother Gerard; Sermon 26 Song of Songs
1139	Bernard's sermons to monks: *Lenten Sermons on the Psalm 'He who dwells'*
1139/40	Bernard's public discourse to students and scholars in Paris; *On Conversion*
1141	William of Saint Thierry persuades Bernard to declare Peter Abelard's teaching on Trinity and Redemption heretical; Bernard condemns Abelard at Council of Sens; Abbot Peter of Cluny effects a reconciliation between Abelard and Bernard
c.1142	Aelred begins to order his writings for the treatise *Mirror of Charity*

1145	A former monk of Clairvaux becomes Pope Eugenius III
1146	Bernard begins to advocate and motivate a second crusade
1147–1150	Second Crusade a disaster
1146/7	Hildegard of Bingen petitions Bernard to support her writings
1147/8	Writings of Hildegard of Bingen approved by Eugenius III and Bernard at the Synod of Trier
1147	Aelred elected Abbot of Rievaulx
c.1148–1152	Bernard writes a treatise addressed to Eugenius III on the papal task, *Five Books on Consideration: Advice to a Pope*
1148	Death of William of Saint Thierry; death of Bernard's friend Archbishop Malachy of Armagh at Clairvaux; Bernard writes *Life of Malachy*
1148–1153	Bernard's revision of his greatest works; including the liturgical sermons
1151	Archbishop Eskil of Lund visits Clairvaux; a close friend of Bernard and Clairvaux
1152	Election of Frederick (Barbarossa) as King of Germany
1153	Bernard's final journey to bring peace to the citizens of Metz
1153	20 August, Bernard's death at Clairvaux
1155	Coronation of Frederick Barbarossa as Holy Roman Emperor
1159	Election of Pope Alexander III begins 18-year schism between emperor and pope; Barbarossa excommunicated for support of anti-pope, Victor IV

CHRONOLOGY OF THE LIFE AND TIMES OF BERNARD OF CLAIRVAUX

1164–1167   Aelred of Rievaulx writes a spiritual treatise, *On Spiritual Friendship*

1167   Death of Aelred of Rievaulx

1174   Bernard canonised by Pope Alexander III

BIBLIOGRAPHY

PRIMARY SOURCES IN TRANSLATION

Aelred of Rievaulx (2010) *Spiritual Friendship*. Translated by L. C. Braceland. Edited and Introduction by M. L. Dutton. (Cistercian Fathers series, 5) Collegeville: Liturgical Press.

— (1990) *The Mirror of Charity*. Translated by E. Connor. Introduction and Notes by C. Dumont (Cistercian Fathers series, 17) Kalamazoo: Cistercian Publications.

Augustine (1901) *The Confessions of St. Augustine*. Translated by E. E. Pusey. London: J. M. Dent.

— (1963) *Saint Augustine the Trinity*. Translated by S. McKenna (The Fathers of the Church. A New Translation, 45). Washington: The Catholic University of America Press.

Benedict (2008) *The Rule of Benedict*. Translated with Introduction and Notes by C. White. London: Penguin Classics.

Bernard of Clairvaux (1971) *On the Song of Songs 1*. Translated by K. Walsh. Introduction by M. Halflants. (The Works of Bernard of Clairvaux, 2. Cistercian Fathers series, 4). Kalamazoo: Cistercian Publications.

— (1976) *On the Song of Songs 2*. Translated by K. Walsh. Introduction by J. Leclercq. (The Works of Bernard of Clairvaux, 3. Cistercian Fathers series, 7). Kalamazoo: Cistercian Publications.

— (1979) *On the Song of Songs 3*. Translated by K. Walsh and I. Edmonds. Introduction by E. Stiegman. (Cistercian Fathers series, 31). Kalamazoo: Cistercian Publications.

— (1980) *On the Song of Songs 4*. Translated by I. Edmonds. Introduction by J. Leclercq. (Cistercian Fathers series, 40). Kalamazoo: Cistercian Publications.

— (1976) *Five Books on Consideration: Advice to a Pope*. Translated by

BIBLIOGRAPHY

J. Anderson and E. Kennan. (Cistercian Fathers series, 37). Kalamazoo: Cistercian Publications.

— (1981) *Sermons on Conversion.* Translated by M.-B. Saïd. (Cistercian Fathers series, 25). Kalamazoo: Cistercian Publications.

— (1981) Lenten Sermons on the Psalm 'He who dwells'. In: *Sermons on Conversion.* Translated by M.-B. Saïd. (Cistercian Fathers series, 25). Kalamazoo: Cistercian Publications, pp. 83–26.

— (1981) On Conversion, A Sermon to Clerics. In: *Sermons on Conversion.* Translated by M.-B. Saïd. (Cistercian Fathers series, 25). Kalamazoo: Cistercian Publications, pp. 11–79.

— (1987) *Bernard of Clairvaux: Selected Works.* Translated and foreword by G. Evans. Preface by E. Cousins. Introduction by J. Leclercq. (The Classics of Western Spirituality). New York: Paulist Press.

— (1987) On Humility and Pride. *Bernard of Clairvaux: Selected Works.* Translated and Foreword by G. Evans. Preface by E. Cousins. Introduction by J. Leclercq. (The Classics of Western Spirituality). New York: Paulist Press, pp. 99–141.

— (1987) On Loving God. *Bernard of Clairvaux: Selected Works.* Translated and foreword by G. Evans. Preface by E. Cousins. Introduction by J. Leclercq. (The Classics of Western Spirituality). New York: Paulist Press, pp. 173–205.

— (1988) *On Grace and Free Choice.* Translated by D. O'Donovan. Introduction by B. McGinn. Kalamazoo: Cistercian Publications.

— (1991) *Sermons for the Summer Season: Liturgical Sermons from Rogationtide and Pentecost.* Translated, with an Introduction by B. Kienzle and J. Jarzembowski. (Cistercian Fathers series, 53). Kalamazoo: Cistercian Publications.

— (1998) *The Letters of St Bernard of Clairvaux.* Translated by B. James. Introduction by B. Kienzle. London: Burns and Oates.

— (1993) *The Life of Malachy.* In: P. Matarasso, *The Cistercian World: Monastic Writings of the Twelfth Century.* Translated and edited with introduction by P. Matarasso. (Penguin Classics). London: Penguin Group.

— (1993) *An Apologia for Abbot William.* In: P. Matarasso, *The Cistercian World: Monastic Writings of the Twelfth Century.* Translated and edited with introduction by P. Matarasso. (Penguin Classics). London: Penguin Group.

Dante (2012) *The Divine Comedy*. Translated and edited with introduction by R. Kirkpatrick. (Penguin Classics). London: Penguin Group.

Isaac of Stella (1993) *Two Sermons*. In: P. Matarasso, *The Cistercian World: Monastic Writings of the Twelfth Century*. Translated and edited with introduction by P. Matarasso. (Penguin Classics). London: Penguin Group.

Walter Daniel (1993) *The Life of Aelred*. In: P. Matarasso, *The Cistercian World: Monastic Writings of the Twelfth Century*. Translated and edited with introduction by P. Matarasso. (Penguin Classics). London: Penguin Group.

William of Saint Thierry (1993) *Vita Prima*. In: P. Matarasso, *The Cistercian World: Monastic Writings of the Twelfth Century*. Translated and edited with introduction by P. Matarasso. (Penguin Classics). London: Penguin Group.

SECONDARY SOURCES

Botterill, S. (1994) *Dante and the Mystical Tradition: Bernard of Clairvaux in the Commedia*. (Cambridge Studies in Medieval Literature, 22). Cambridge: Cambridge University Press.

Bruun, M.B. (2011) Bernard of Clairvaux and the Landscape of Salvation. In: McGuire, B. (ed.) *A Companion to Bernard of Clairvaux* (Brill's Companions to the Christian Tradition, 25). Leiden: Koninklijke Brill NV, pp. 249–278.

Campbell, J. (2012) *Light on Prophecy: Retrieving Word and Spirit in Today's Church*. Milton Keynes: Paternoster.

Carmichael, E.D.H. (2004) *Friendship: Interpreting Christian Love*. London: T.&T. Clark International.

Casey, M. (2011) Reading Saint Bernard: The Man, the Medium, the Message. In: B. McGuire (ed.) *A Companion to Bernard of Clairvaux*. (Brill's Companions to the Christian Tradition, 25). Leiden: Koninklijke Brill NV, pp. 62–107.

Chenu, M.-D. (1968) *Nature, Man, and Society in the Twelfth Century: Essays on New Theological Perspectives in the Latin West*. Selected, edited and translated by J. Taylor and L. Little. Chicago: University of Chicago Press.

Deanesly, M. (1954) *A History of the Medieval Church 590–1500*. (8th edn) London: Methuen & Co. Ltd.

BIBLIOGRAPHY

Dronke, P. (1974) *Fabula: Explorations into the uses of myth in medieval Platonism.* (Mittellateinische Studien und Texte. Band 9). Leiden.

Dumont, C. (1999) *Pathway of Peace. Cistercian Wisdom according to Saint Bernard.* Translated by E. Connor, E. Kalamazoo: Cistercian Publications.

Elder, E. (2011) Bernard and William of Saint Thierry. In: McGuire, B. (ed.) *A Companion to Bernard of Clairvaux* (Brill's Companions to the Christian Tradition, 25). Leiden: Koninklijke Brill NV, pp. 108–132.

Flanagan, S. (1989) *Hildegard of Bingen 1098–1179: A Visionary Life.* Routledge: London.

France, J. (2011) The Heritage of Saint Bernard in Medieval Art. In: McGuire, B. (ed.) *A Companion to Bernard of Clairvaux* (Brill's Companions to the Christian Tradition, 25). Leiden: Koninklijke Brill NV, pp. 304–346.

Hawkins, Peter, S. (1999) *Dante's Testaments: Essays in Scriptural Imagination.* Standford: Standford University Press.

Holdsworth, C. (2011) Bernard as a Father Abbot. In: McGuire, B. (ed.) *A Companion to Bernard of Clairvaux* (Brill's Companions to the Christian Tradition, 25). Leiden: Koninklijke Brill NV, pp. 169–219.

Kasper, W. (1982) *The God of Jesus Christ.* Translated by M. O'Connell. London: SCM Press Ltd.

Keen, M. (1968) *The Pelican History of Medieval Europe.* Harmondsworth: Penguin Books.

Knowles, D. (1962) *The Evolution of Medieval Thought.* London: Longman.

Lewis, C.S. (1958) *The Allegory of Love: A Study in Medieval Tradition.* Oxford: OUP.

Leclercq, J. (1989) *Women and Saint Bernard of Clairvaux.* Kalamazoo: Cistercian Publications.

Leroux-Dhuys, J.-F. (1998) *Cistercian Abbeys: History and Architecture.* Translated by E. Clegg, C. Higgitt, and M.-N. Ryan. Köln: Könemann.

Matarasso, P. (1993) *The Cistercian World: Monastic Writings of the Twelfth Century.* Translated and edited with introduction by P. Matarasso. (Penguin Classics) London: Penguin Group.

Mews, C. (2011) Bernard of Clairvaux and Peter Abelard. In: McGuire, B. (ed.) *A Companion to Bernard of Clairvaux* (Brill's Companions to the Christian Tradition, 25). Leiden: Koninklijke Brill NV, pp. 133–168.

McGuire, B. (2020) *Bernard of Clairvaux: An Inner Life*. New York: Cornell University Press.

— (ed.) (2011) *A Companion to Bernard of Clairvaux*. (Brill's Companions to the Christian Tradition, 25) Leiden: Koninklijke Brill NV.

— (2011) Bernard's Life and Works: A Review. In: McGuire, B. (ed.) *A Companion to Bernard of Clairvaux* (Brill's Companions to the Christian Tradition, 25). Leiden: Koninklijke Brill NV, pp. 18–61.

Newman, B. (1990) Some Mediaeval Theologians and the Sophia Tradition. The Downside Review. 108 (371). pp. 111–130.

Petersen, J. (1984) The Dialogues of Gregory the Great in their late antique cultural background. (Toronto: Pontifical Institute of Mediaeval Studies. Studies and Texts, 69). Leiden: E.J. Brill.

Pranger, M.B. (2011) Bernard the Writer. In: McGuire, B. (ed.) *A Companion to Bernard of Clairvaux* (Brill's Companions to the Christian Tradition, 25). Leiden: Koninklijke Brill NV, pp. 220 - 248.

Ricoeur, P and Mudge, L. (1981) *Essays on Biblical Interpretation*. London: SPCK.

Schipperges, H. (1998) *The World of Hildegard of Bingen*. Translated by J. Cumming. Tunbridge Wells: Burns & Oates.

Sommerfeldt, J. (1991) *The Spiritual Teachings of Bernard of Clairvaux: An Intellectual History of the Early Cistercian Order*. Kalamazoo: Cistercian Publications.

— (2011) Afterword: Looking back at Bernard. In: McGuire, B. (ed.) *A Companion to Bernard of Clairvaux* (Brill's Companions to the Christian Tradition, 25). Leiden: Koninklijke Brill NV, pp. 369–373.

Watkin-Jones, H. (1922) *The Holy Spirit in the Mediaeval Church: A Study of Christian Teaching concerning The Holy Spirit and His place in the Trinity From the Post-Patristic Age to the Counter-Reformation*. London: The Epworth Press.

Other titles by Jennifer Campbell:

Strengthen Your Core

Prophecy for Anyone

The Way of Prophetic Leadership

Light on Prophecy

Available to purchase from
waverleyabbeyresources.org

WAVERLEY ABBEY COLLEGE

Learn to be the Difference

Equipping people to be the positive impact on society through:

- Nurturing personal growth;
- Delivering academic excellence; and
- Developing pastoral compassion

Courses and resources that equip you to be the difference where you are.

waverleyabbeycollege.ac.uk

WAVERLEY ABBEY TRUST

Love God, Love All

Waverley Abbey Trust is a ministry, equipping you to love God, love your neighbour and love yourself.

Through our portfolio of courses and plethora of resources, you can learn to be the difference in society. Our free Bible reading notes help you to draw closer to Jesus and by living every day with Jesus, we believe you can foster the foundation to help and serve others.

waverleyabbeytrust.org